ABSTRACT

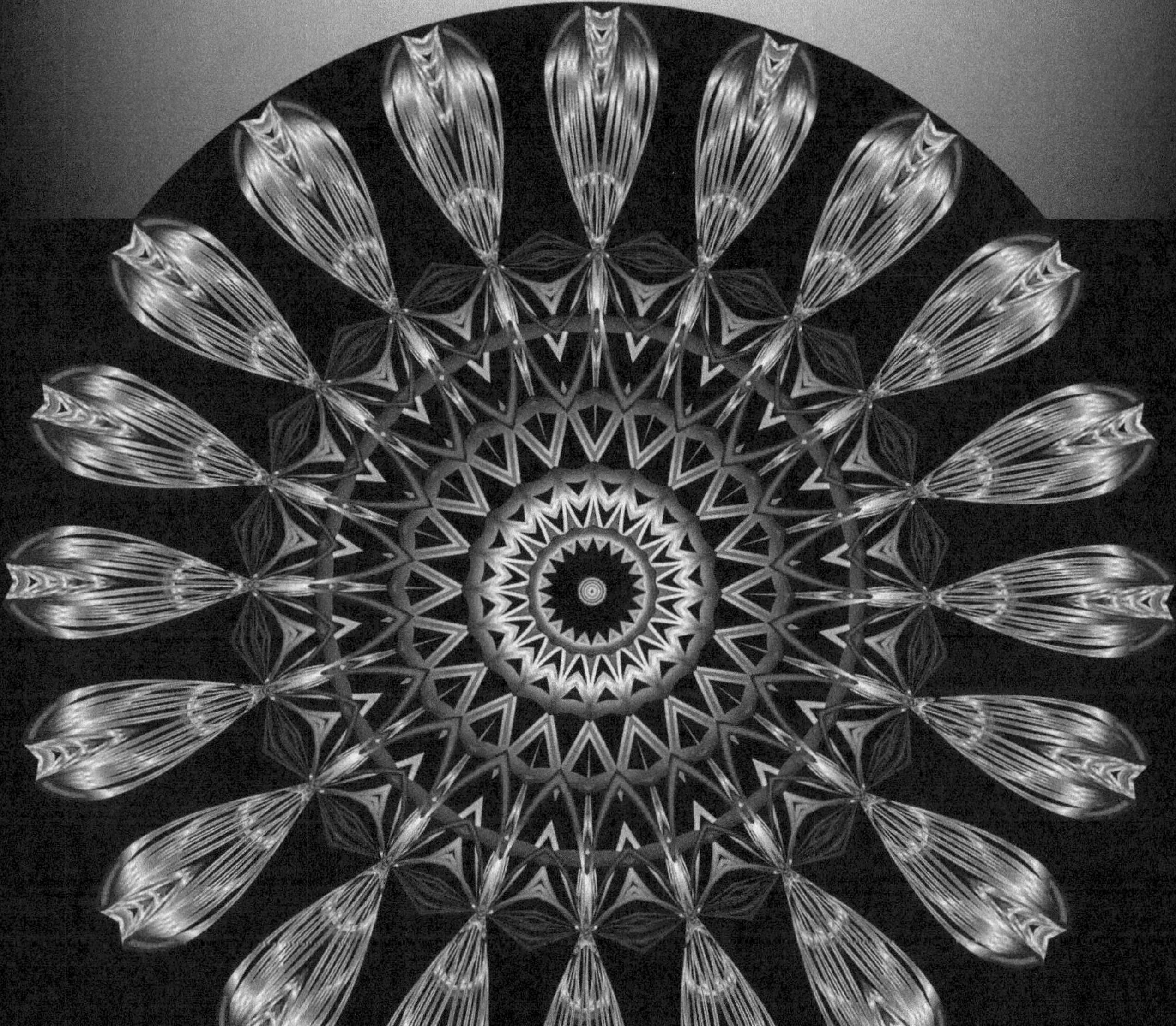

ADULT COLORING BOOK

Lindsey Bright

COPYRIGHT

This book is entirely a work of fiction.

Any resemblance to actual persons, living

or dead, is entirely coincidental.

Lindsey Bright Author

Pandorra Publishing (July 2018)

ISBN: 9781717861368

Amazon Digital Services LLC

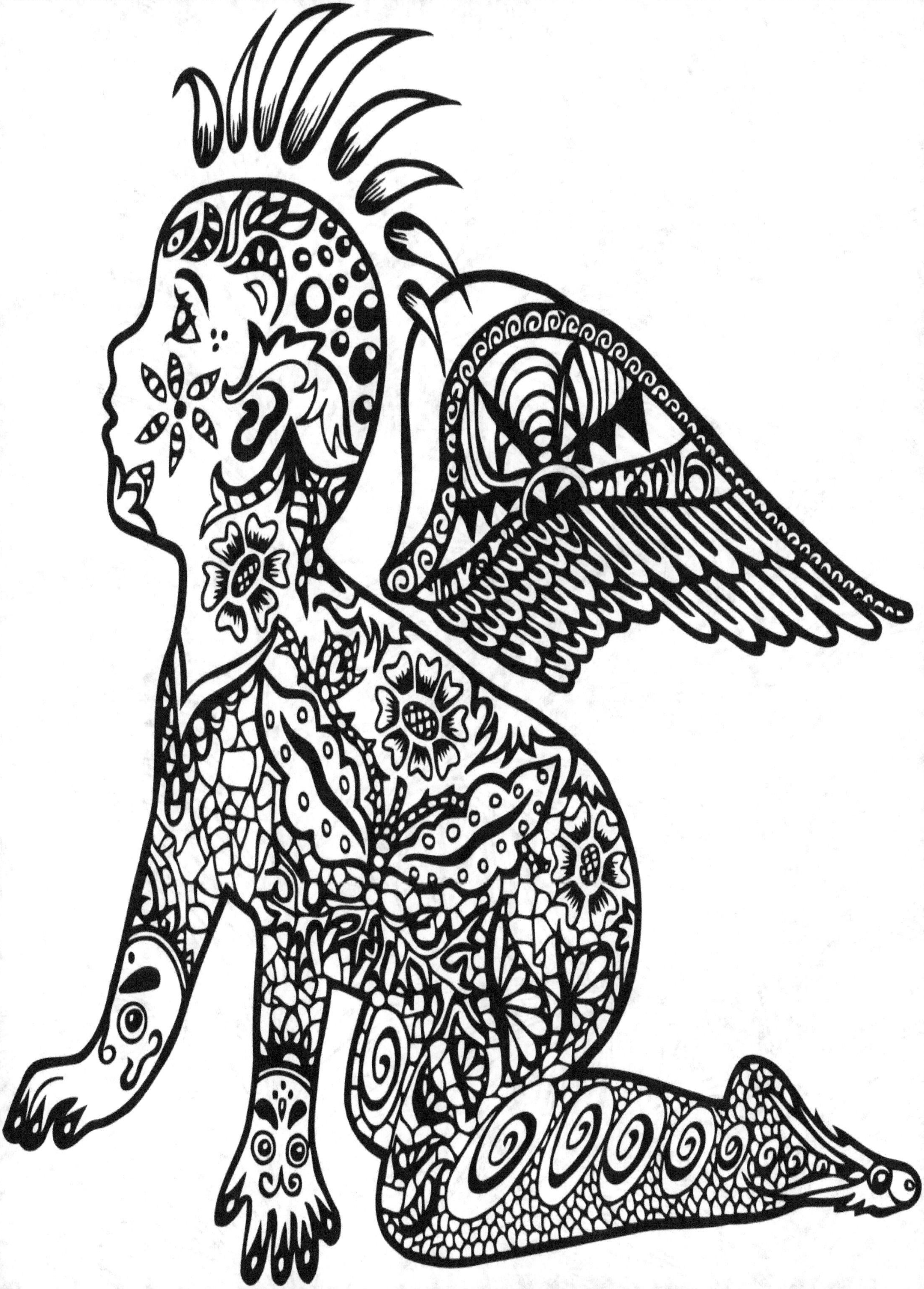

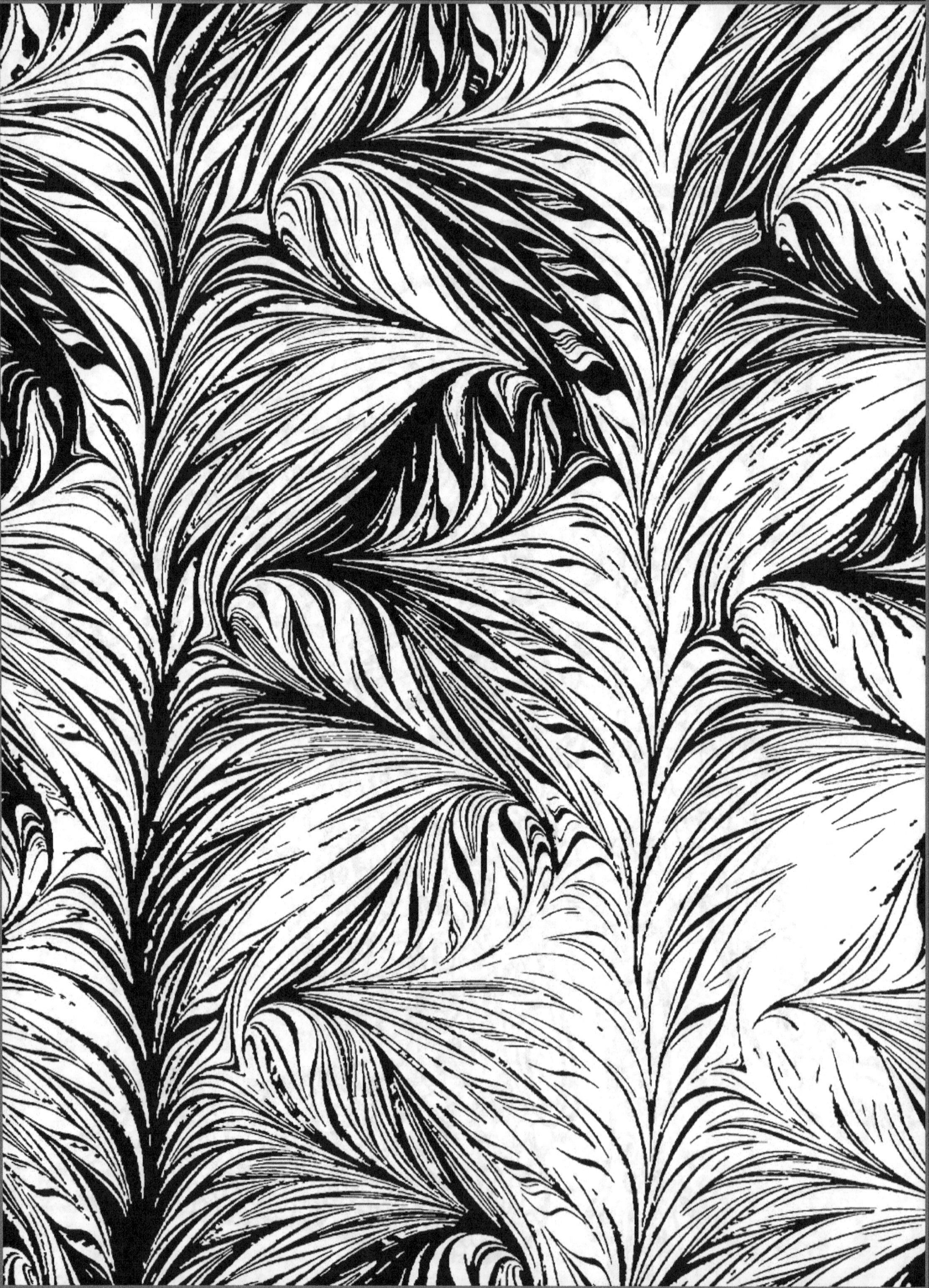

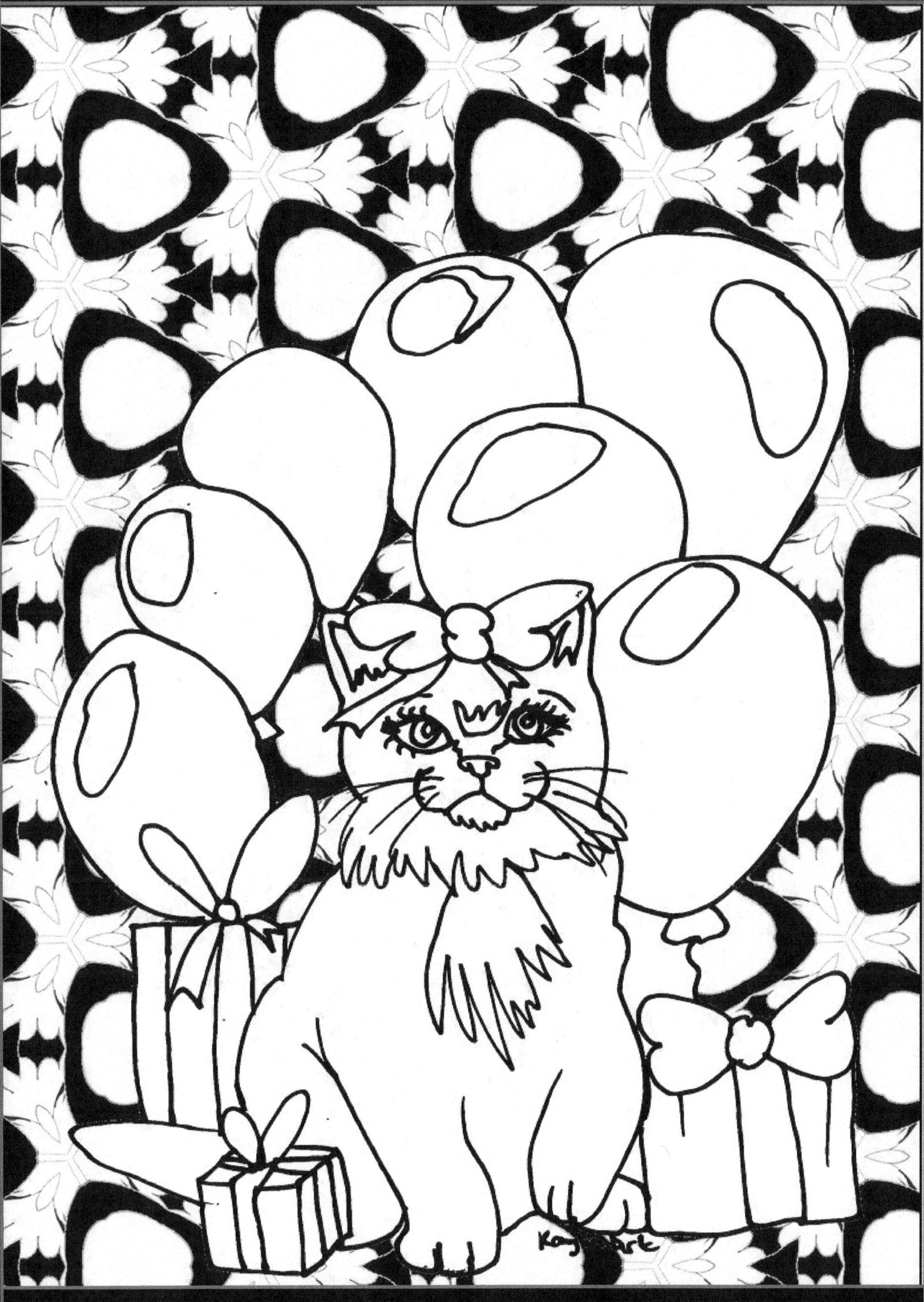

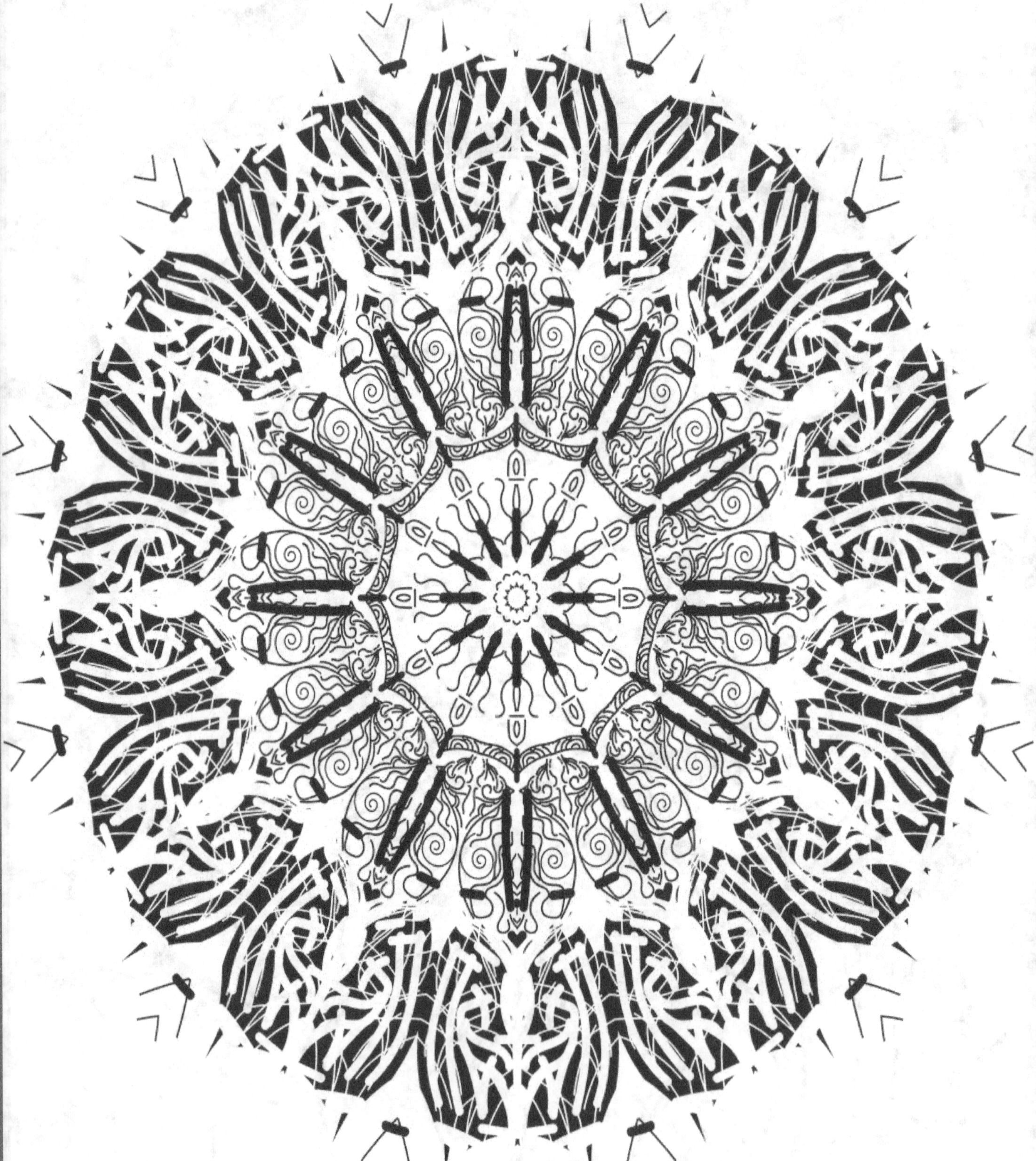

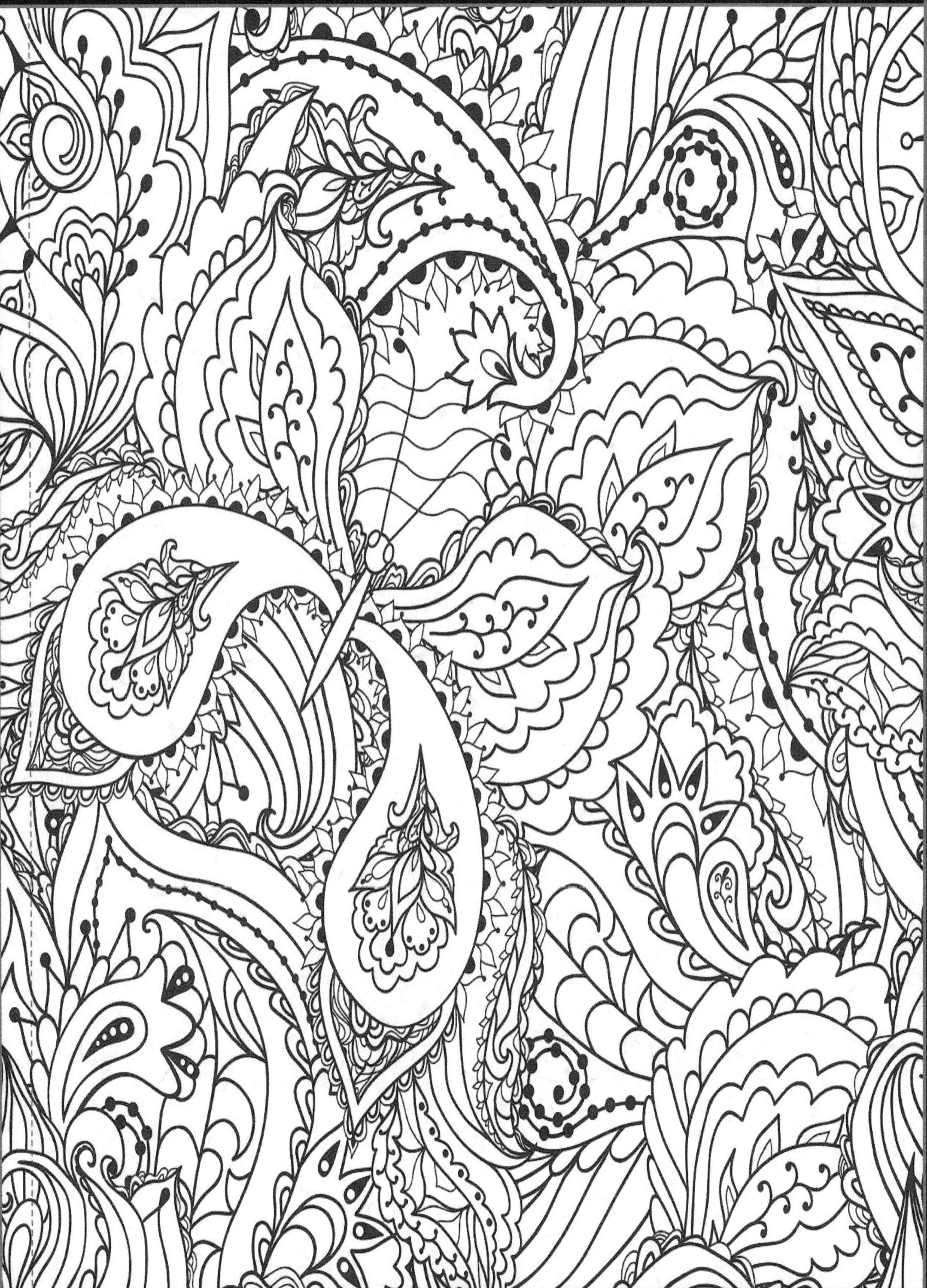

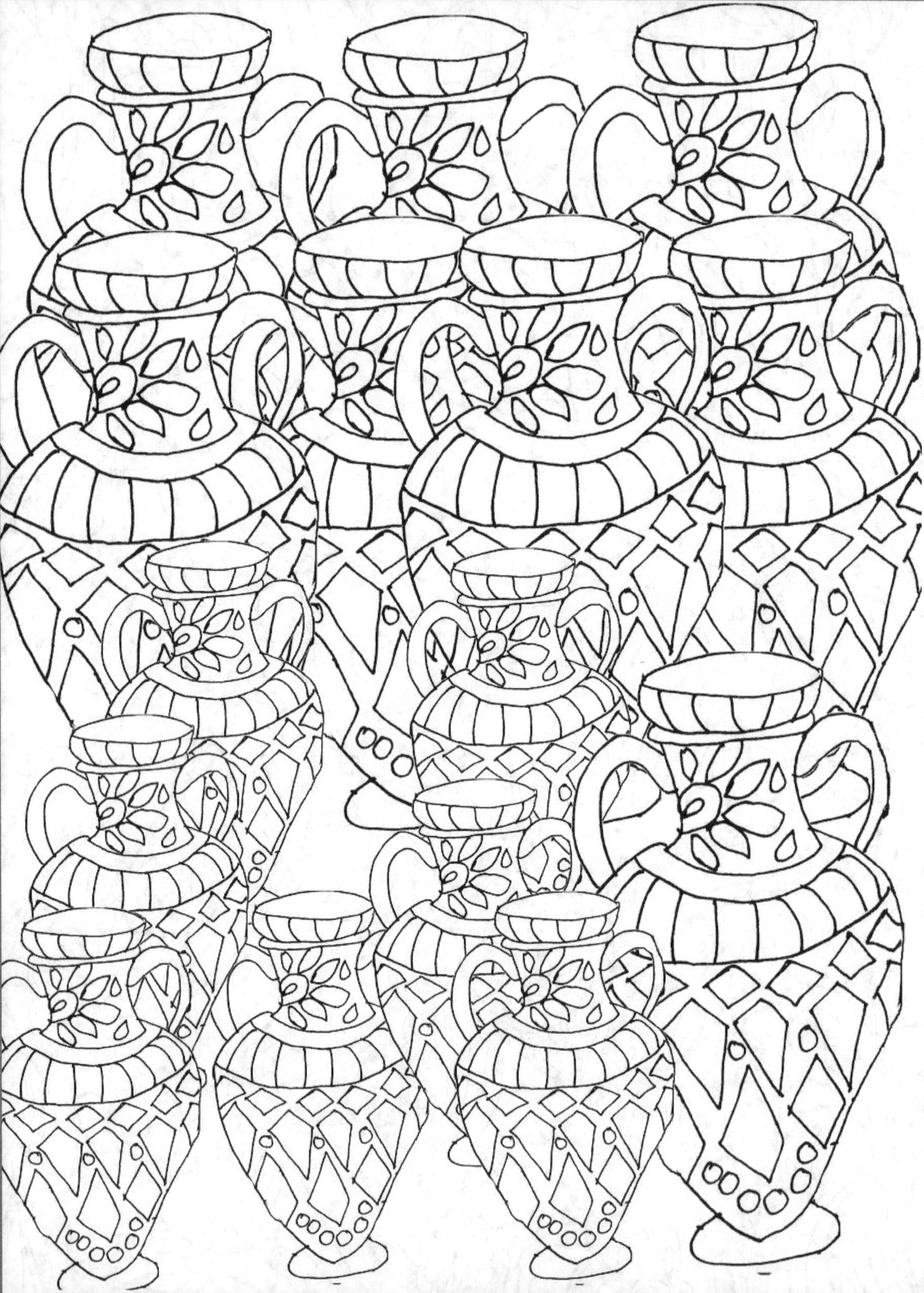

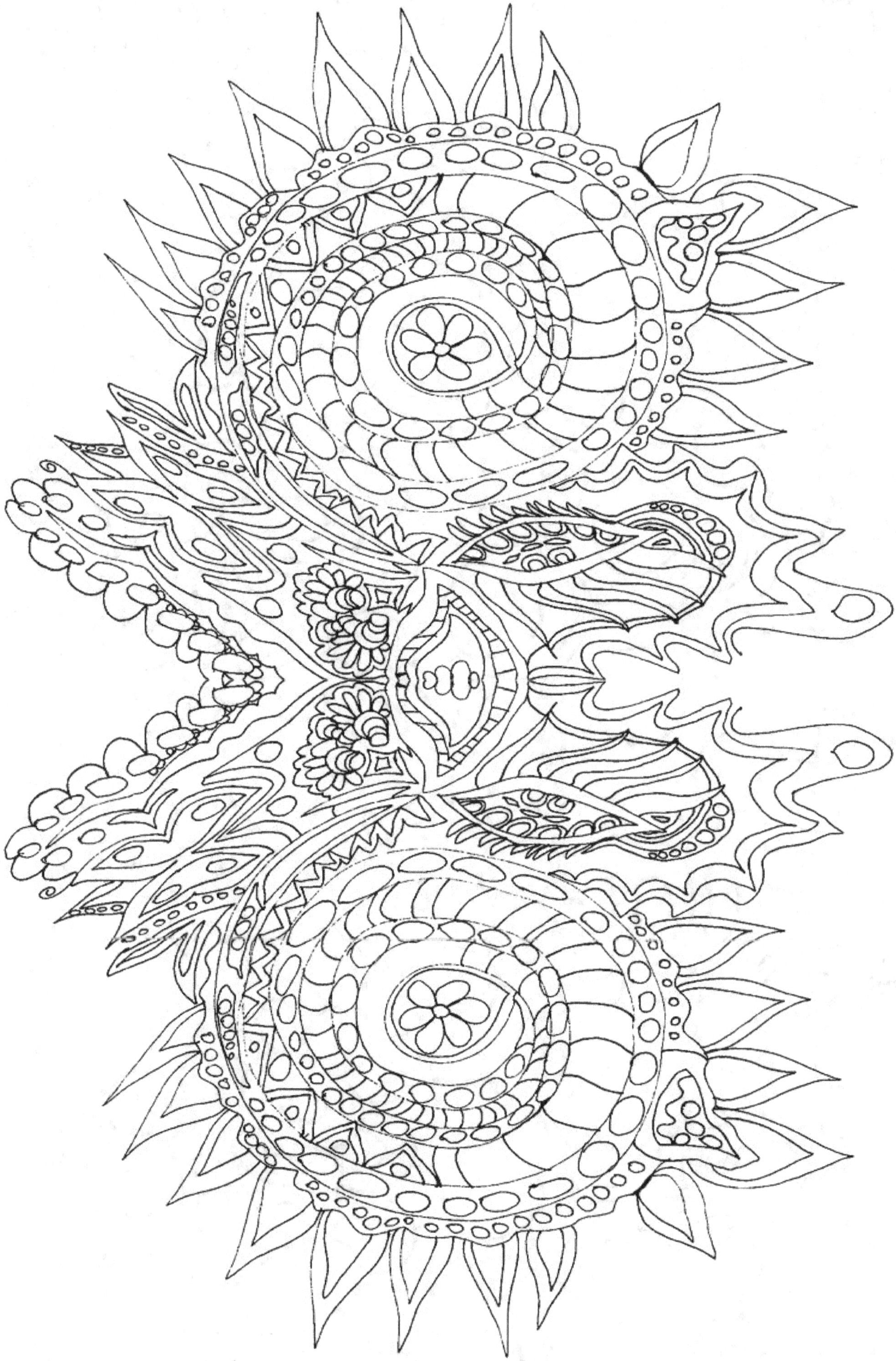

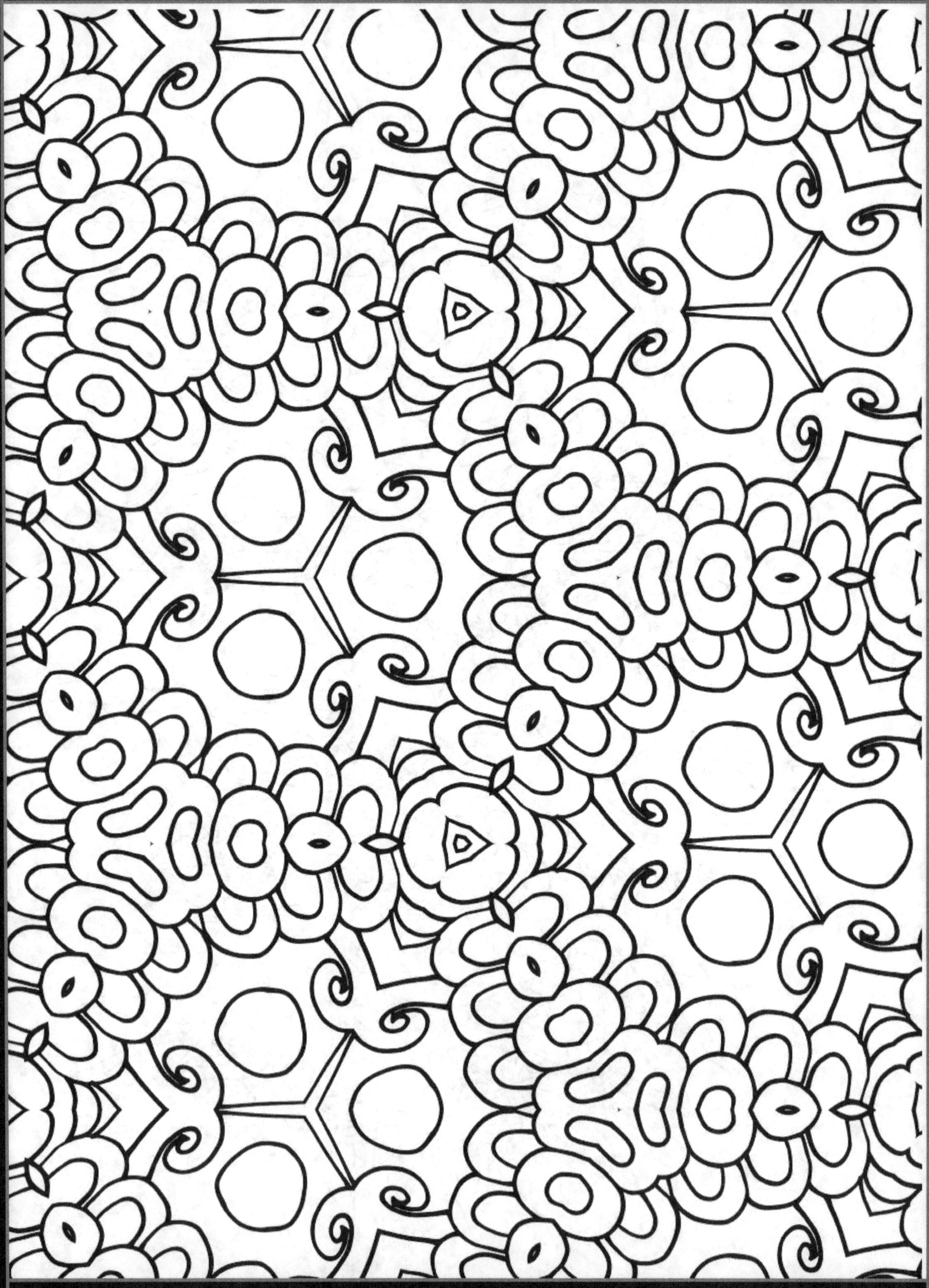

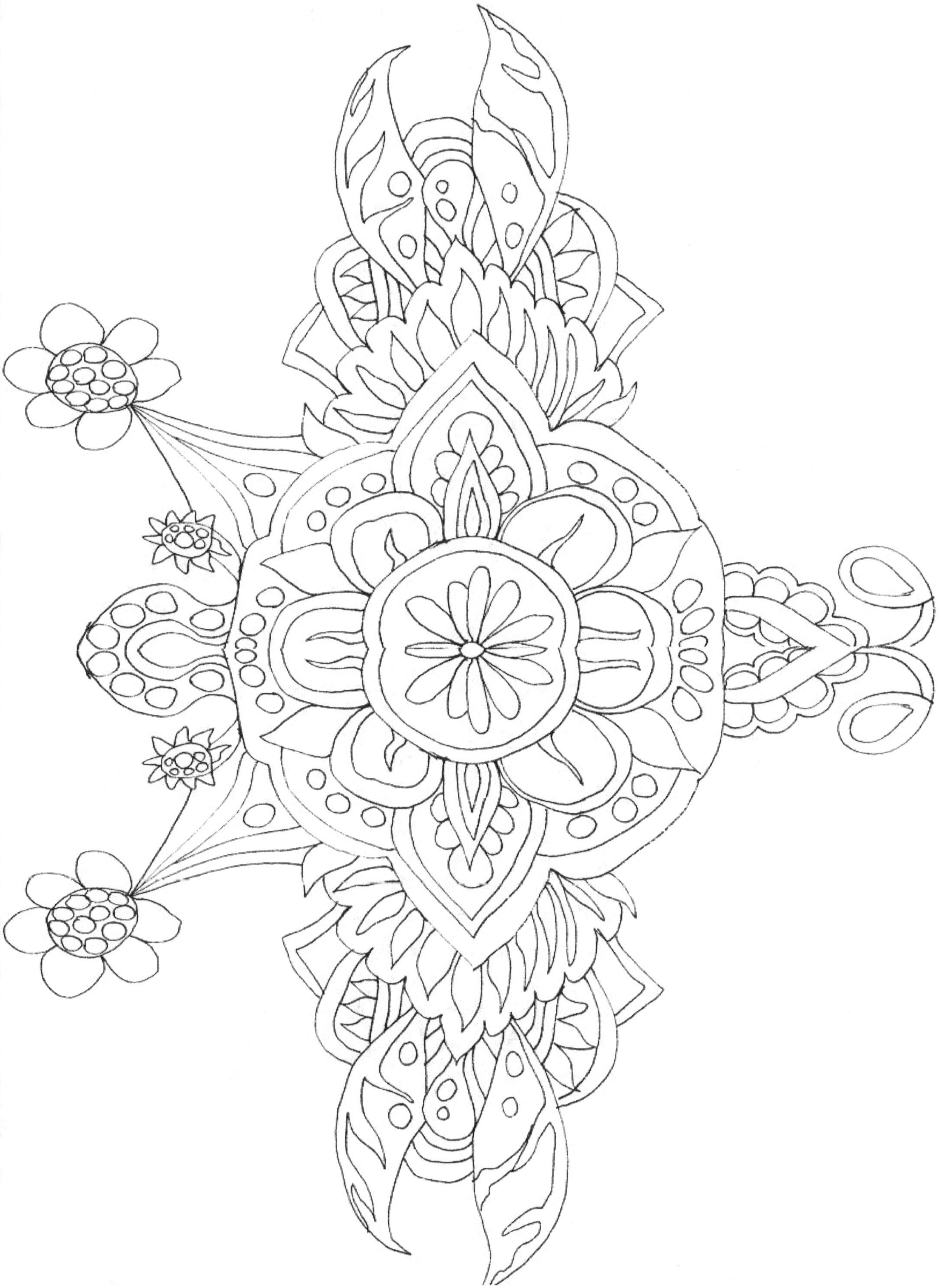

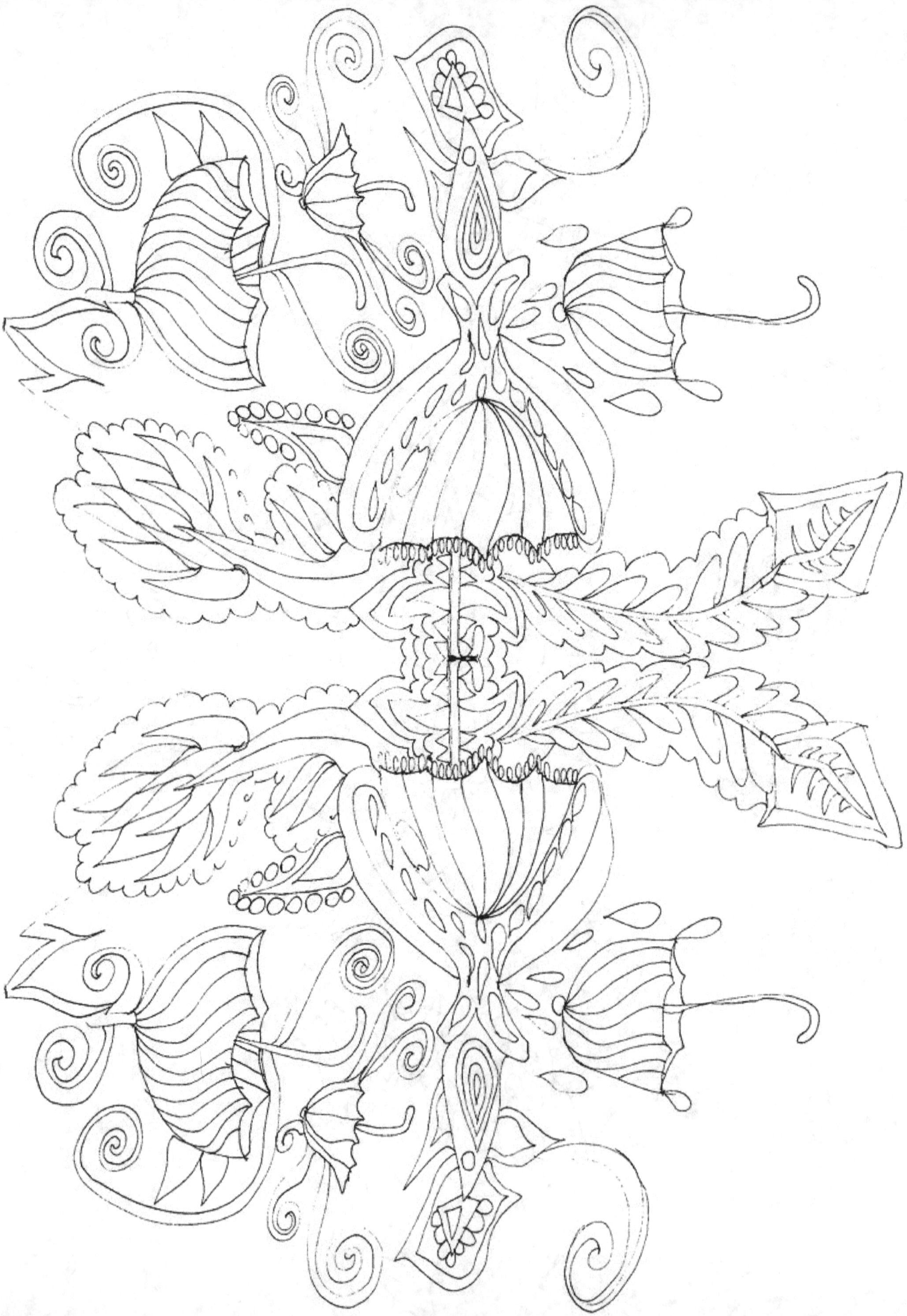

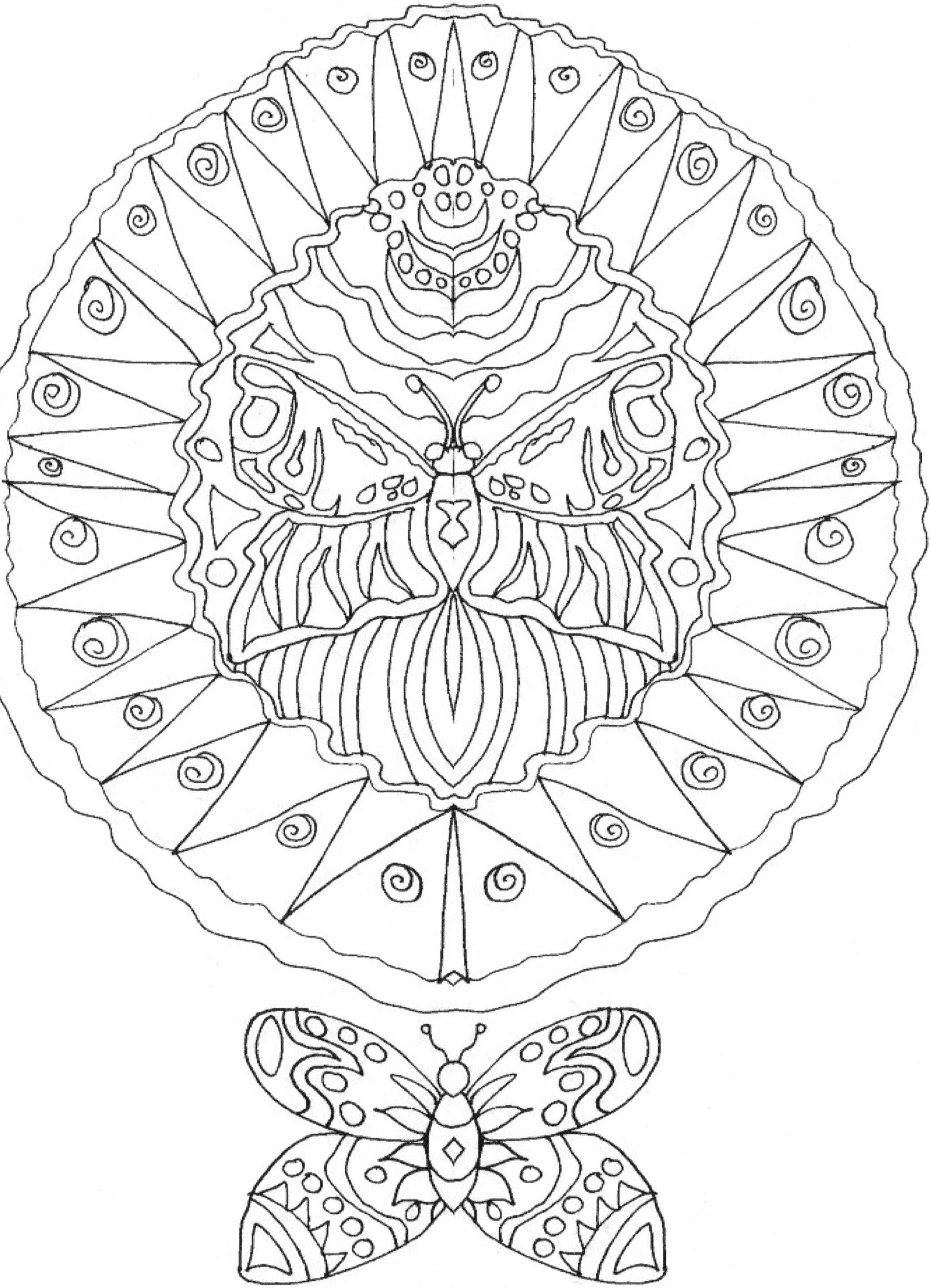

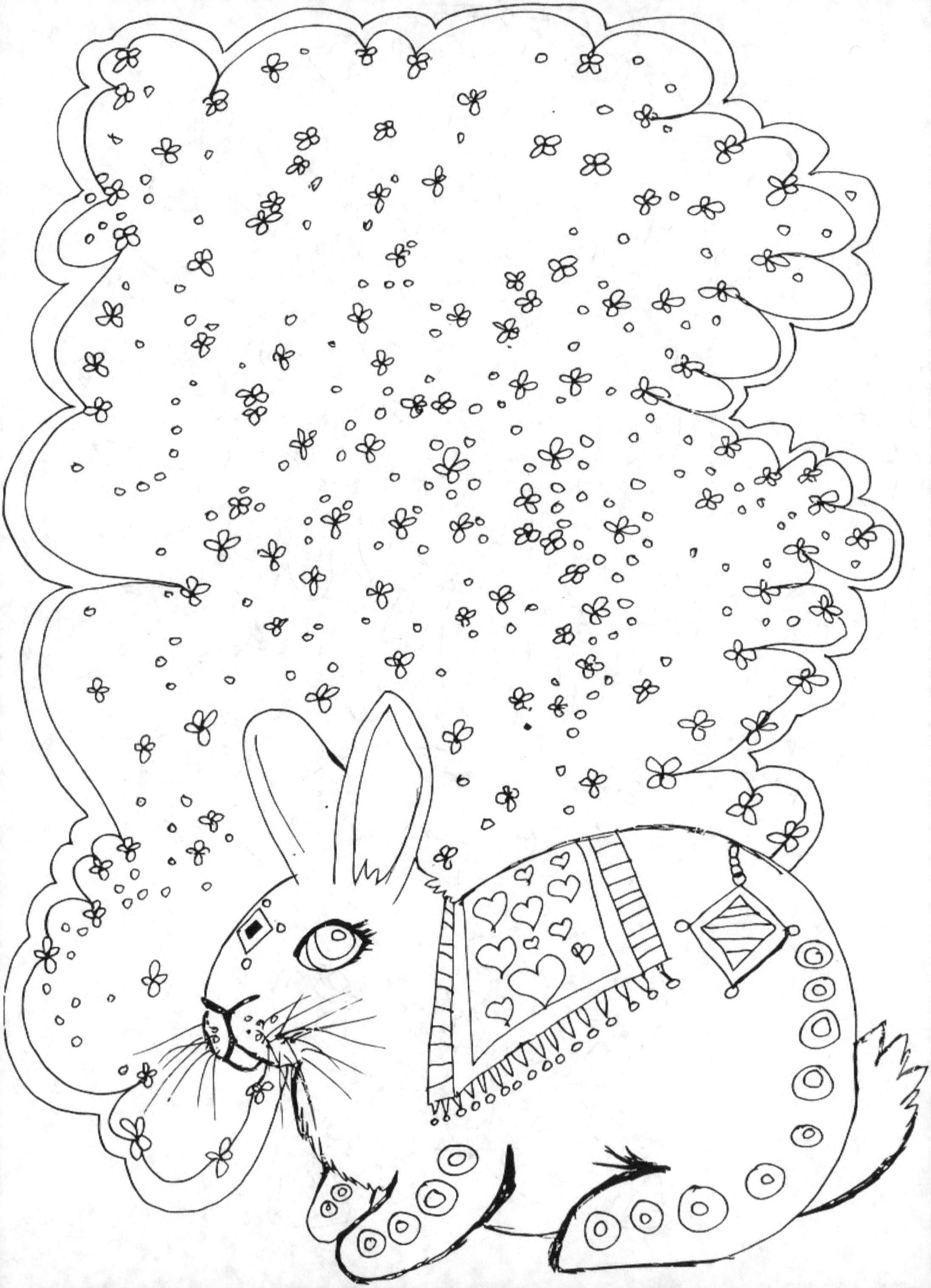

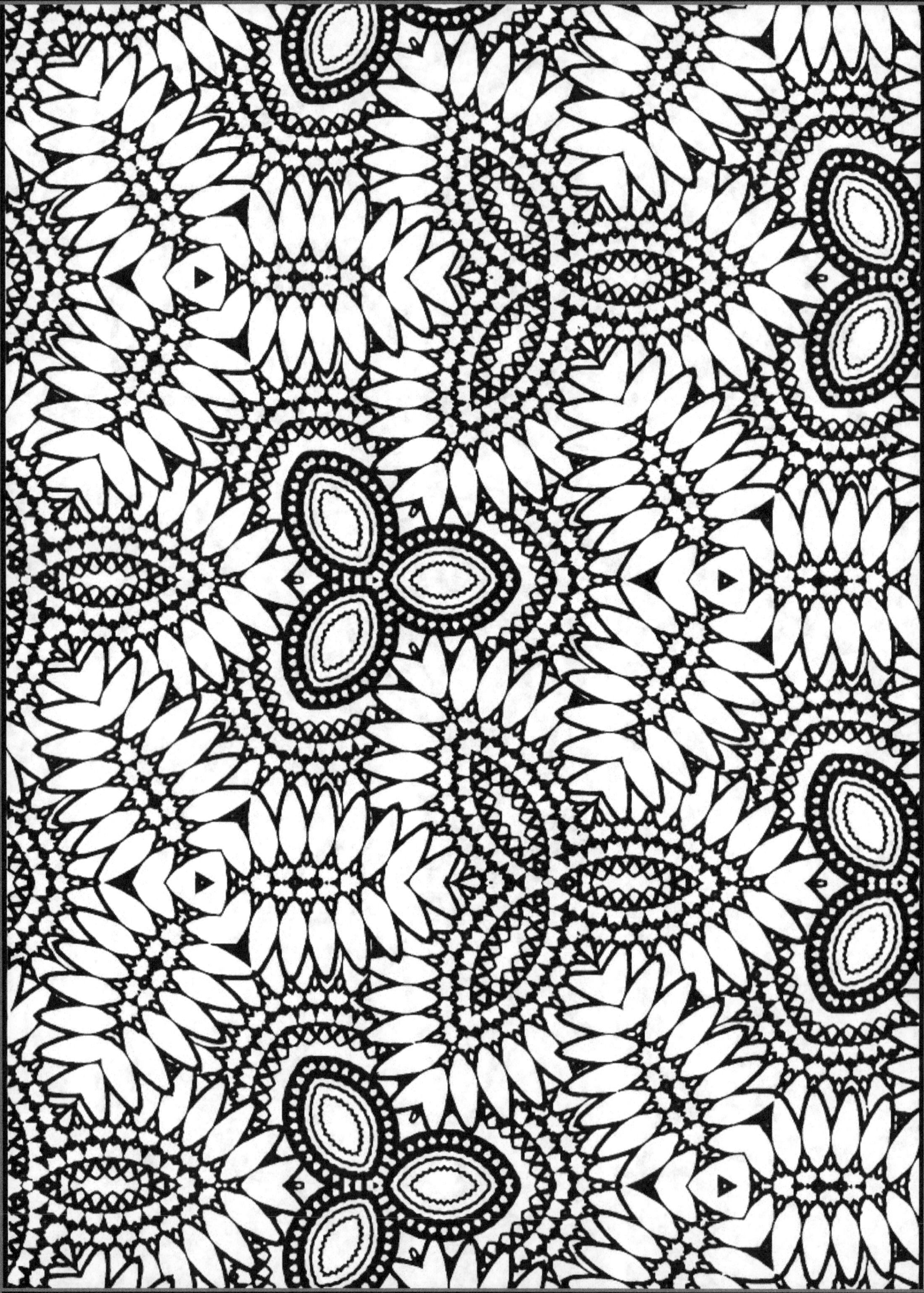

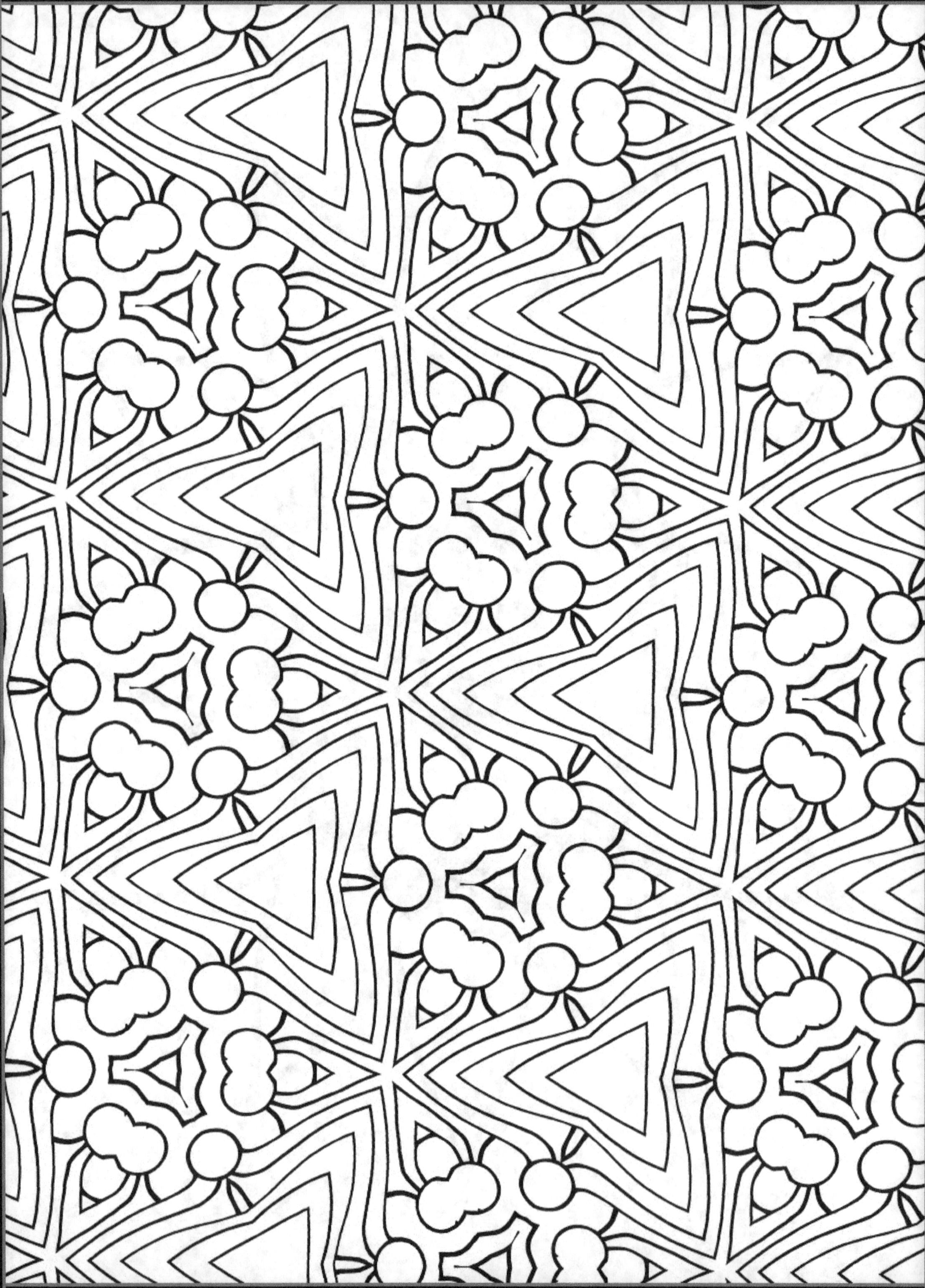

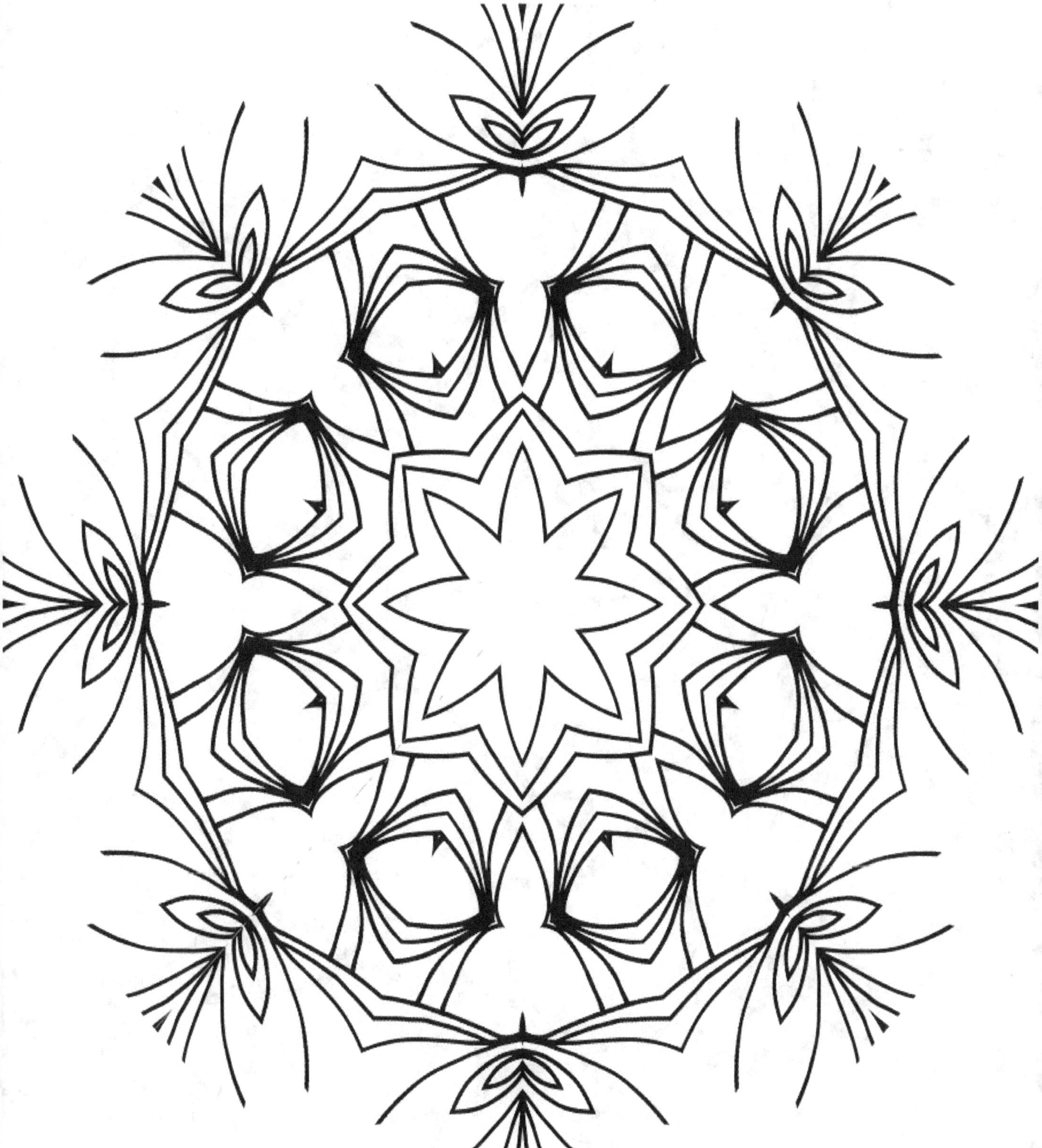

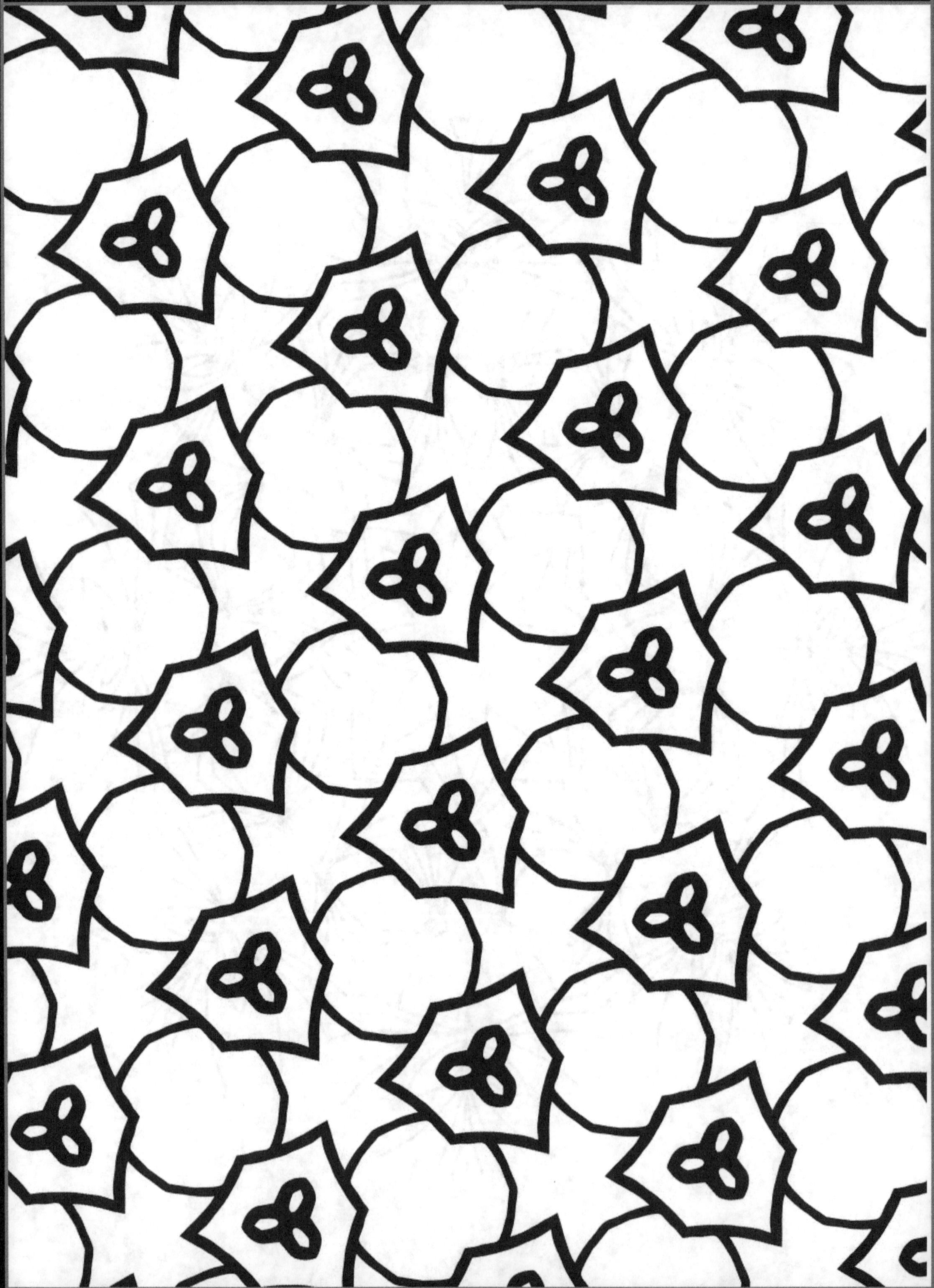

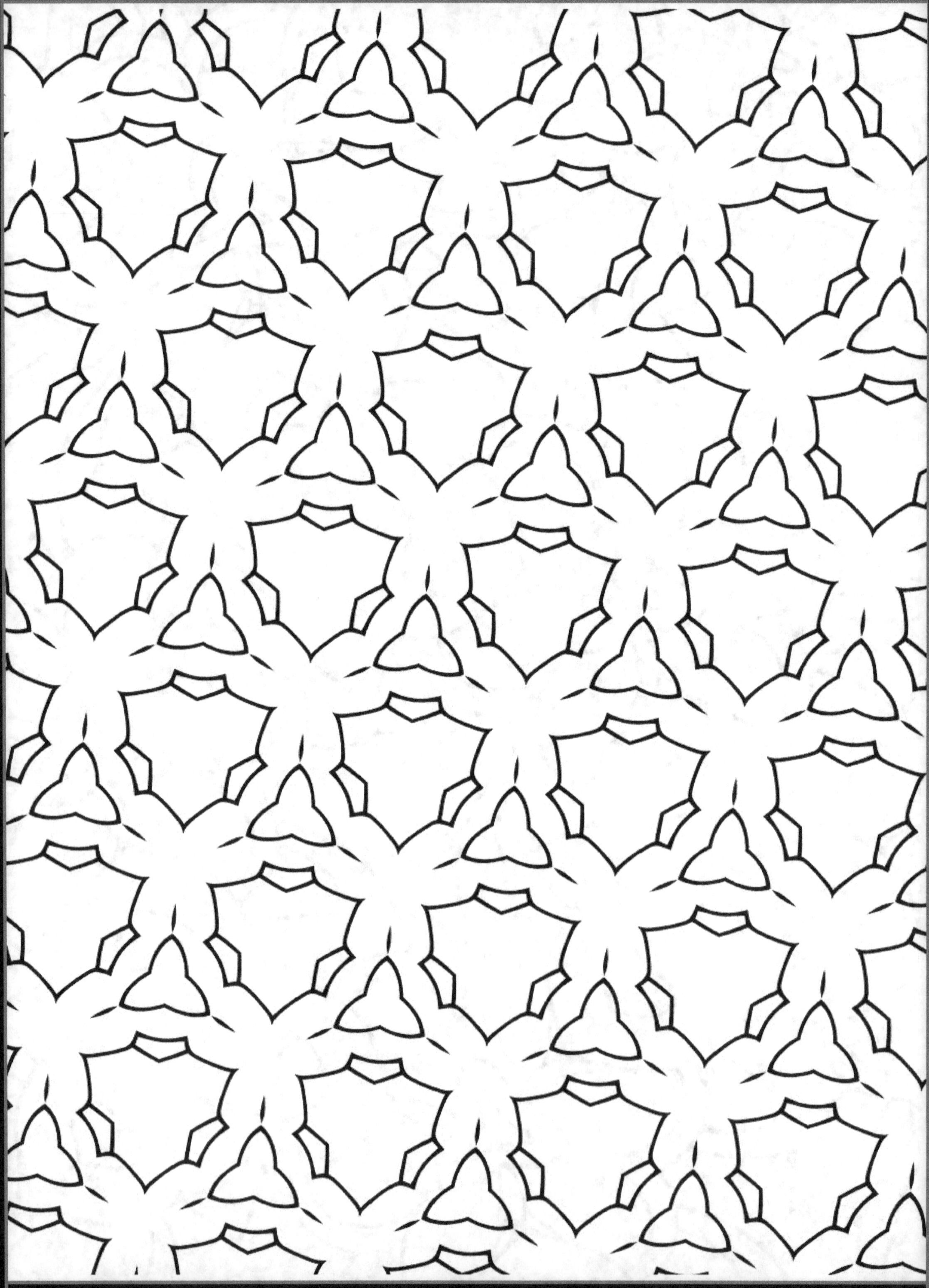

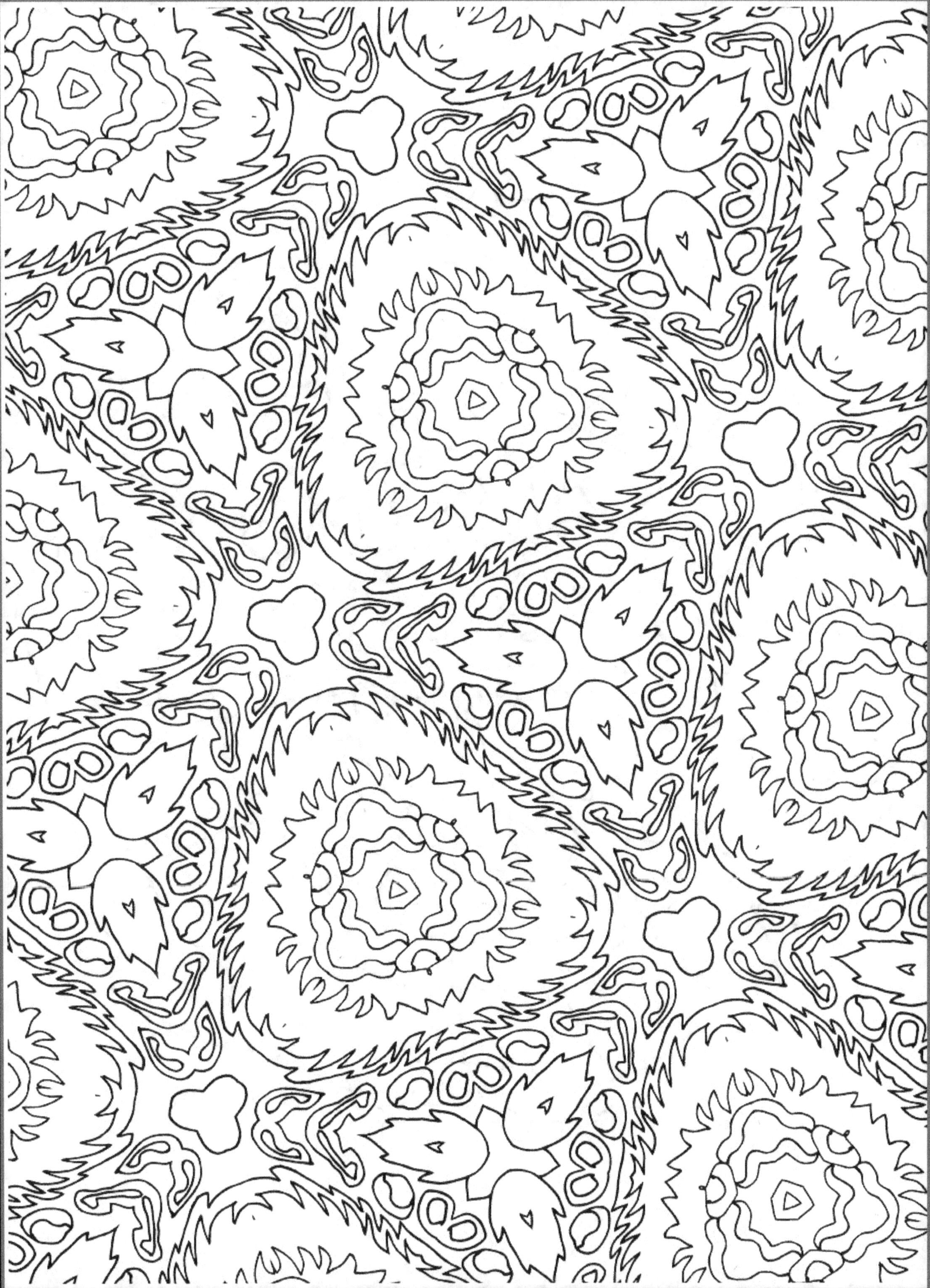

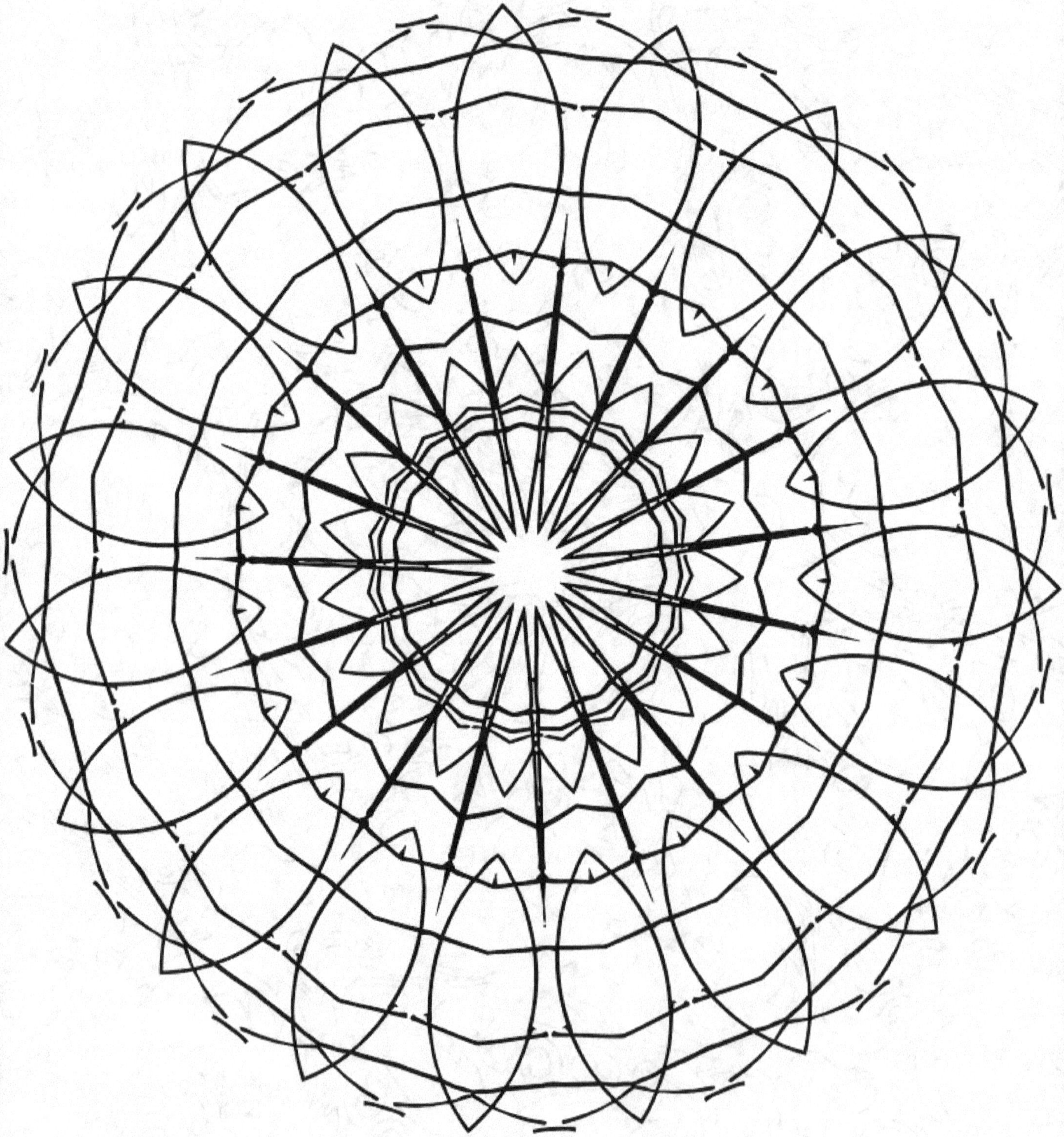

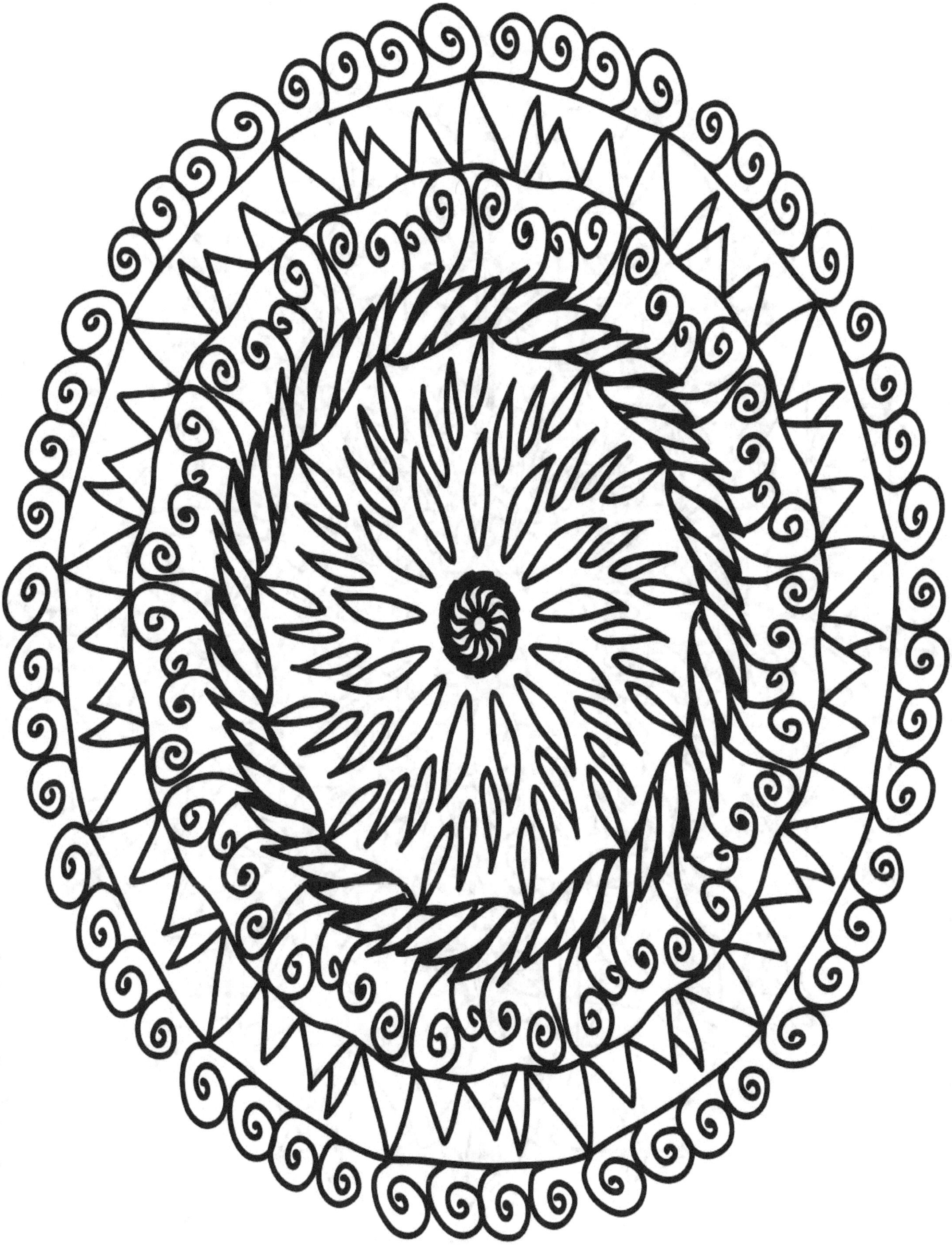

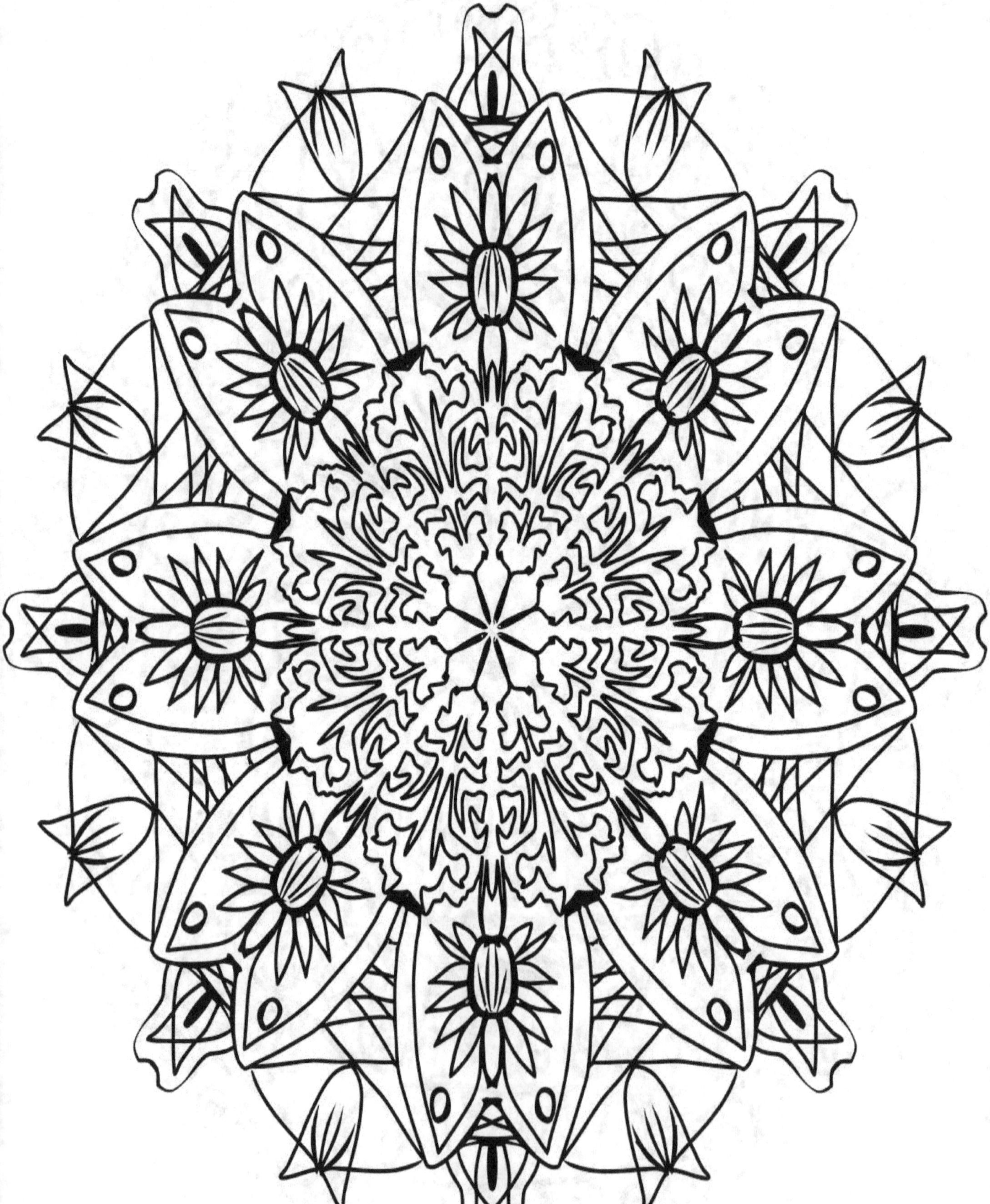

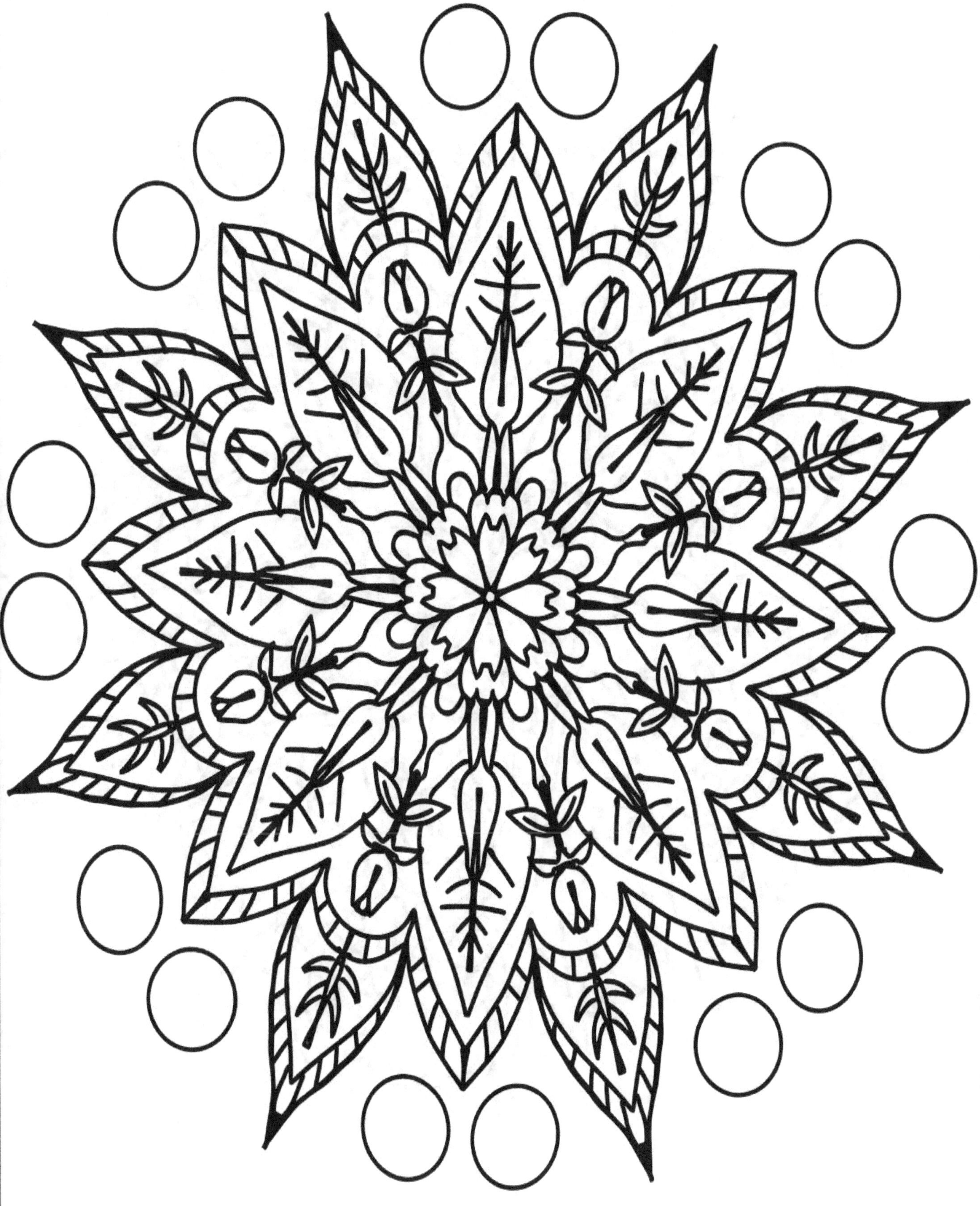

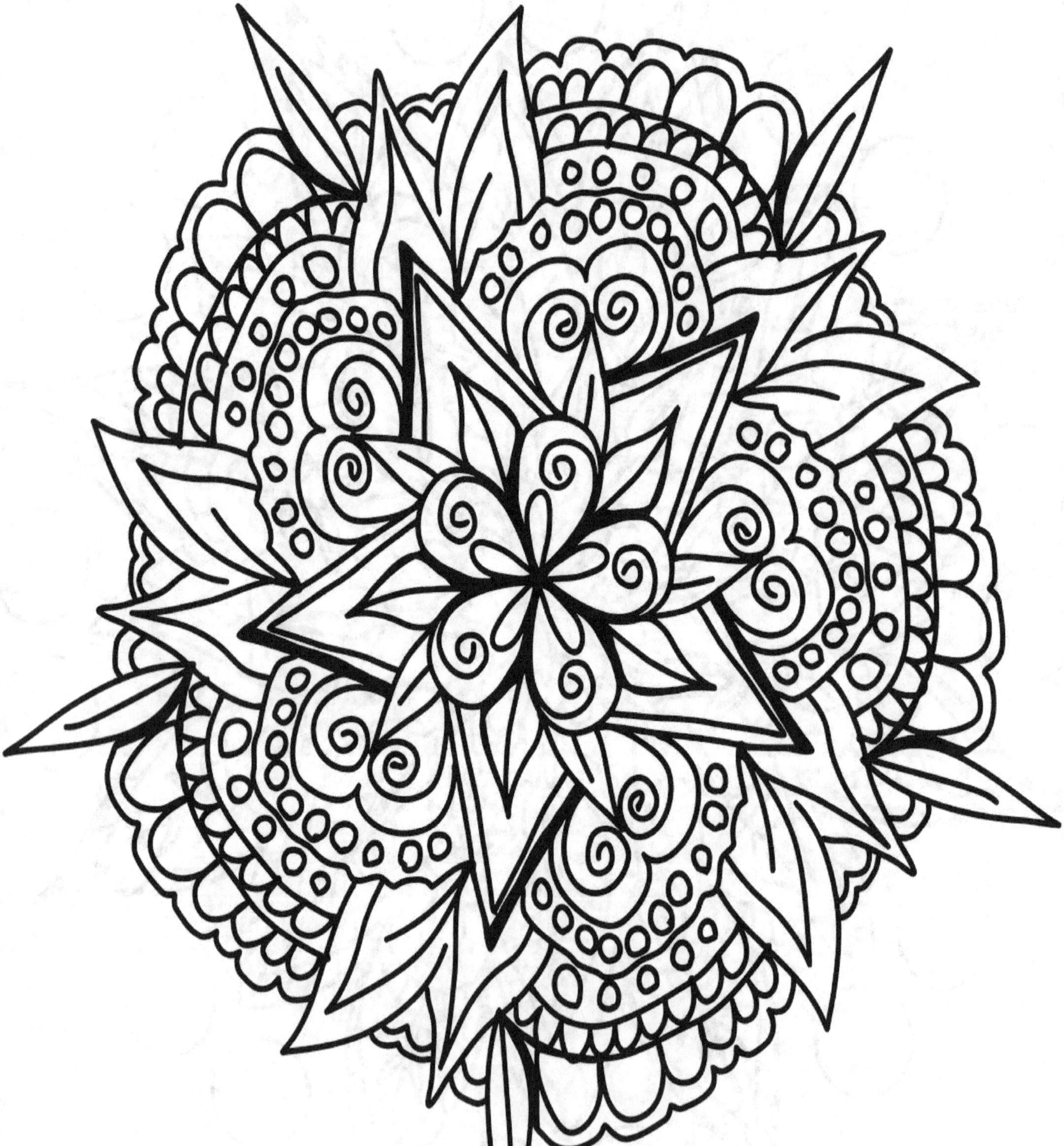

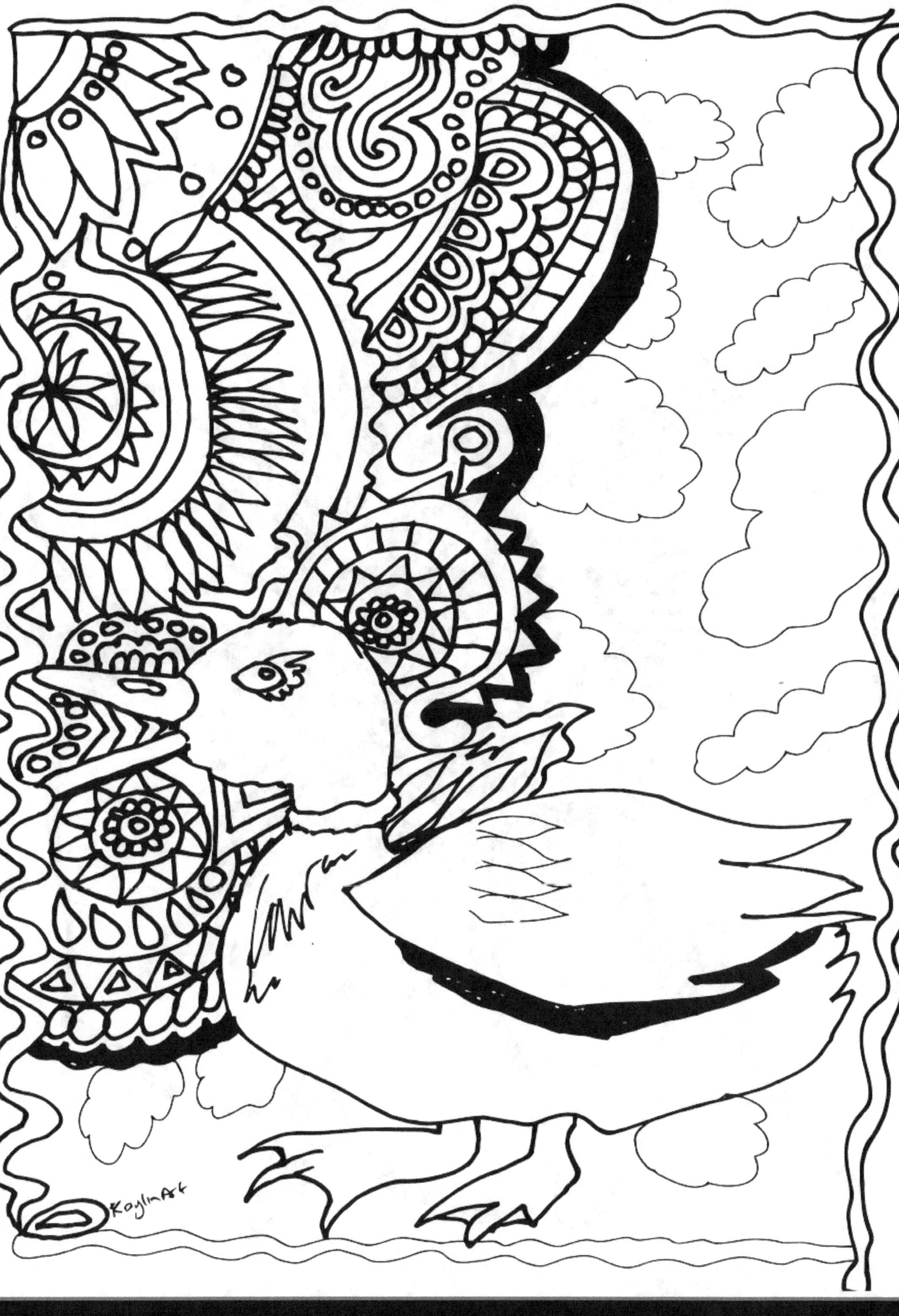
KaylinArt

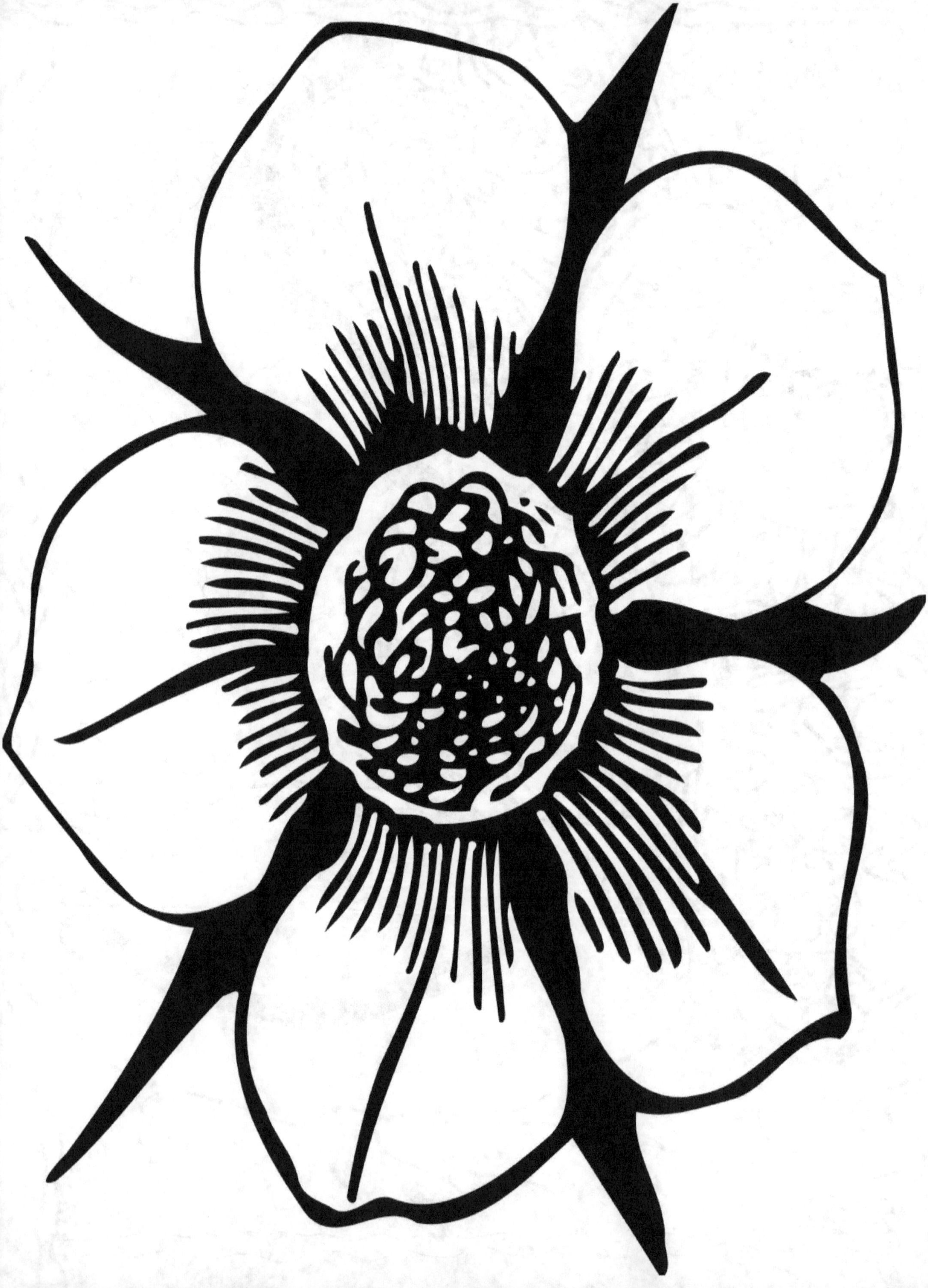

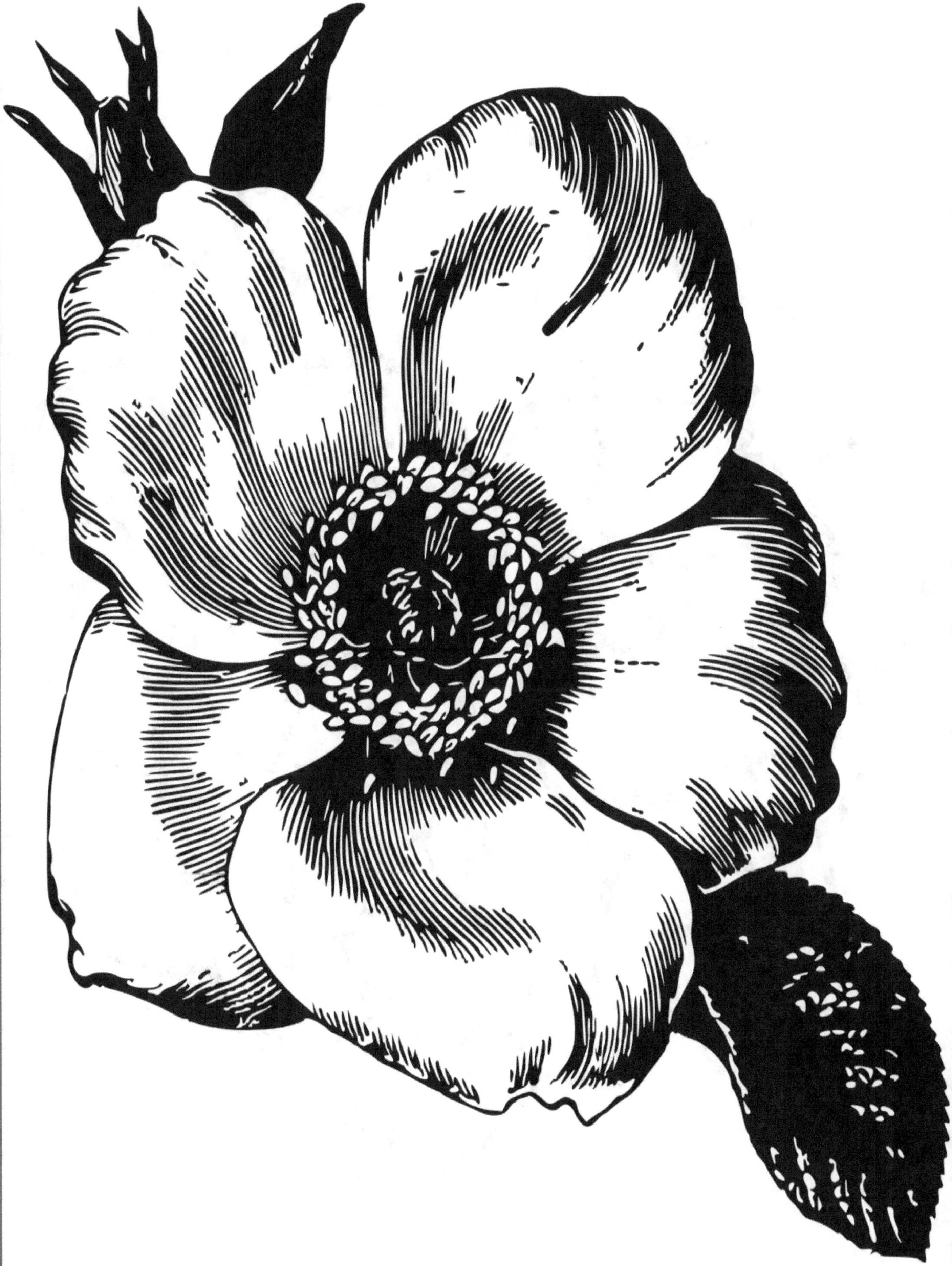

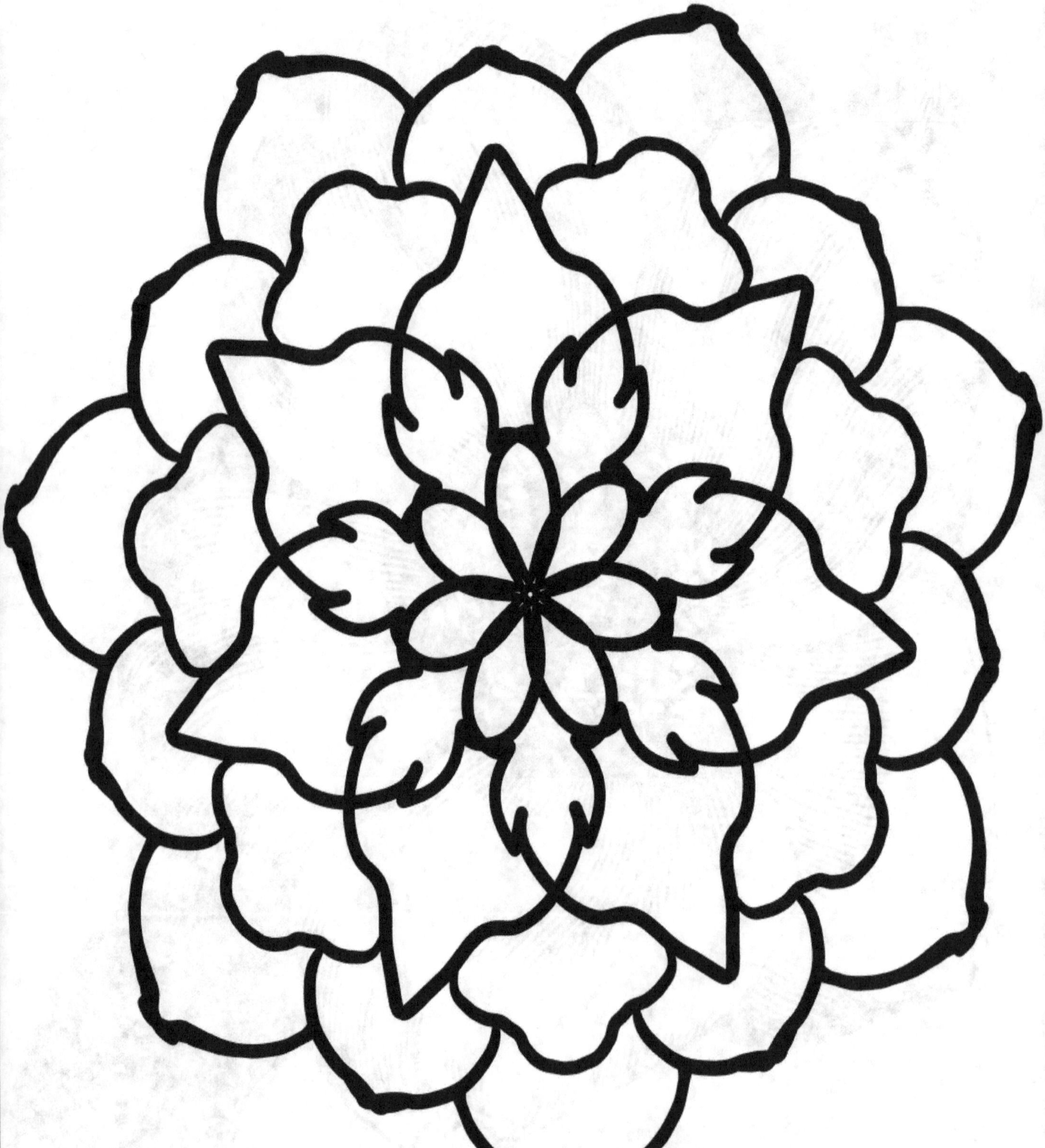

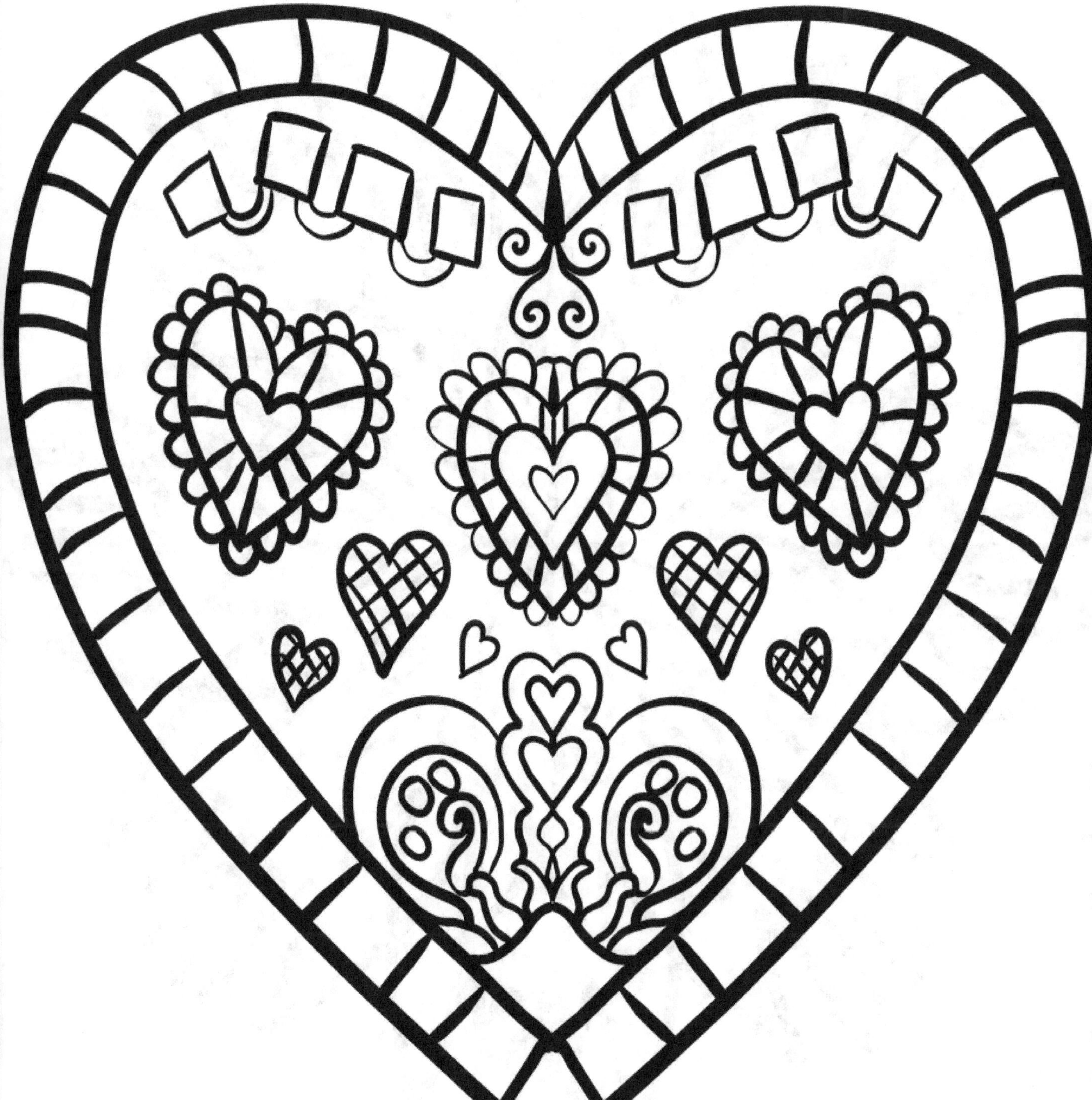

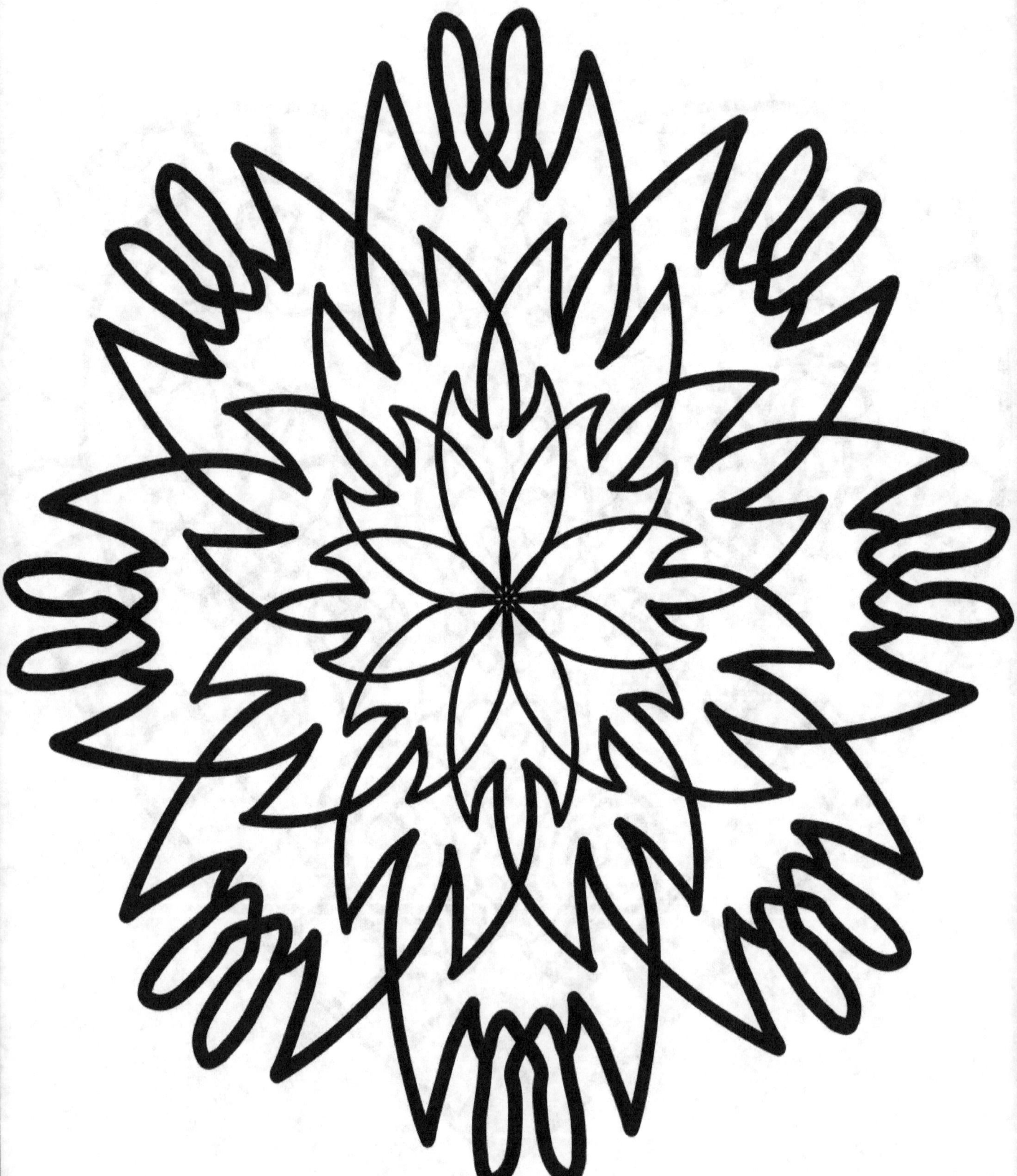

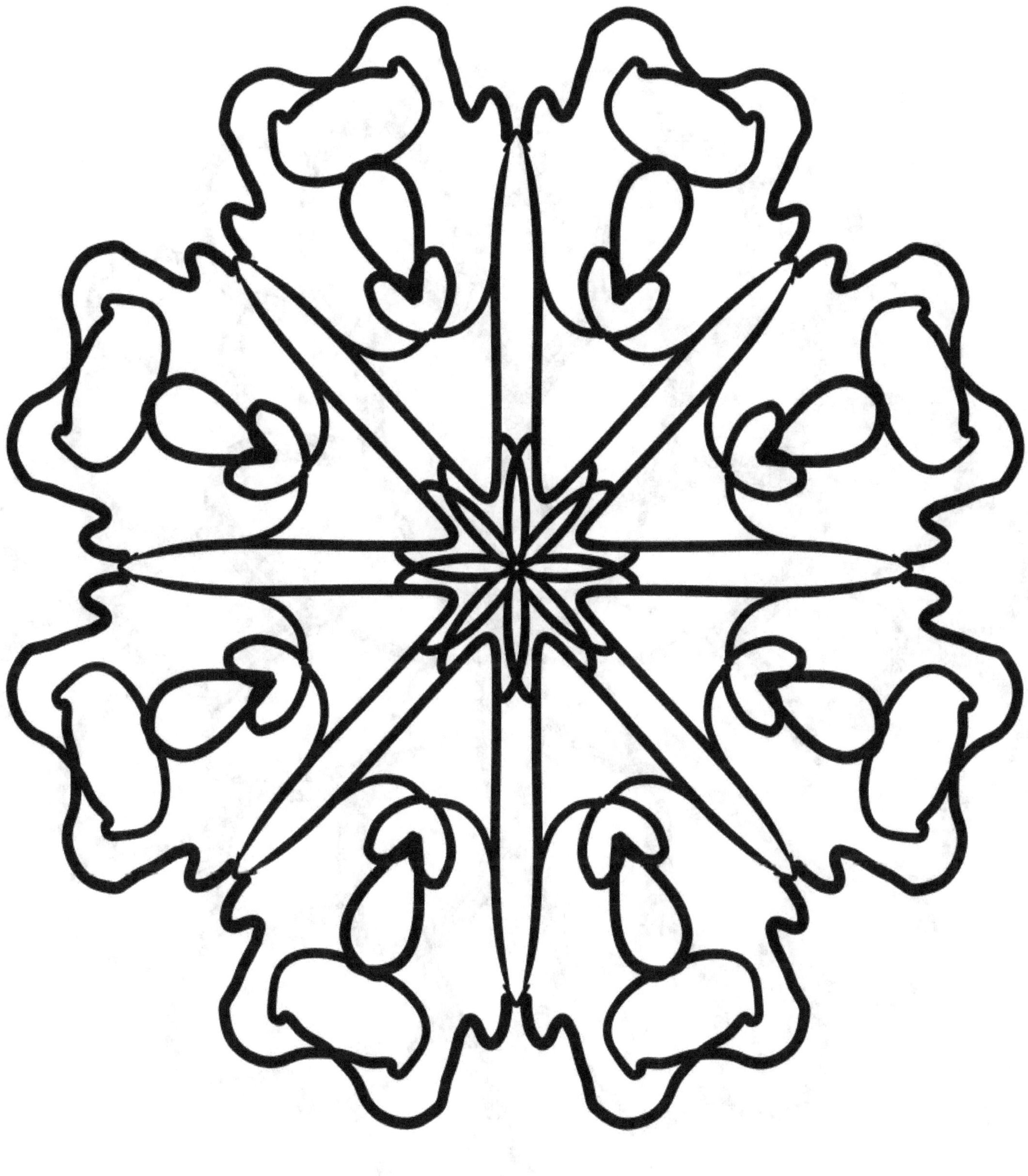

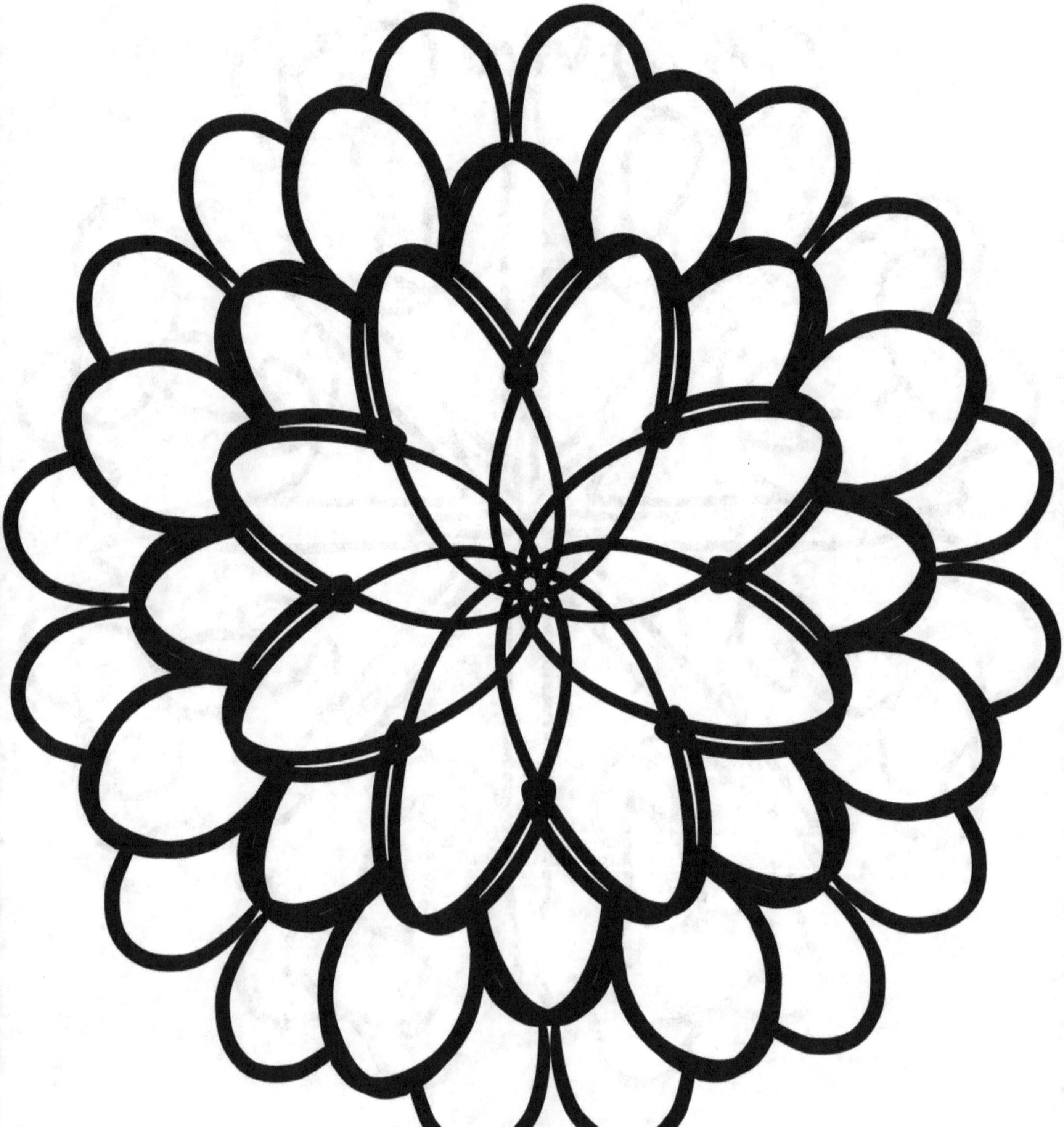

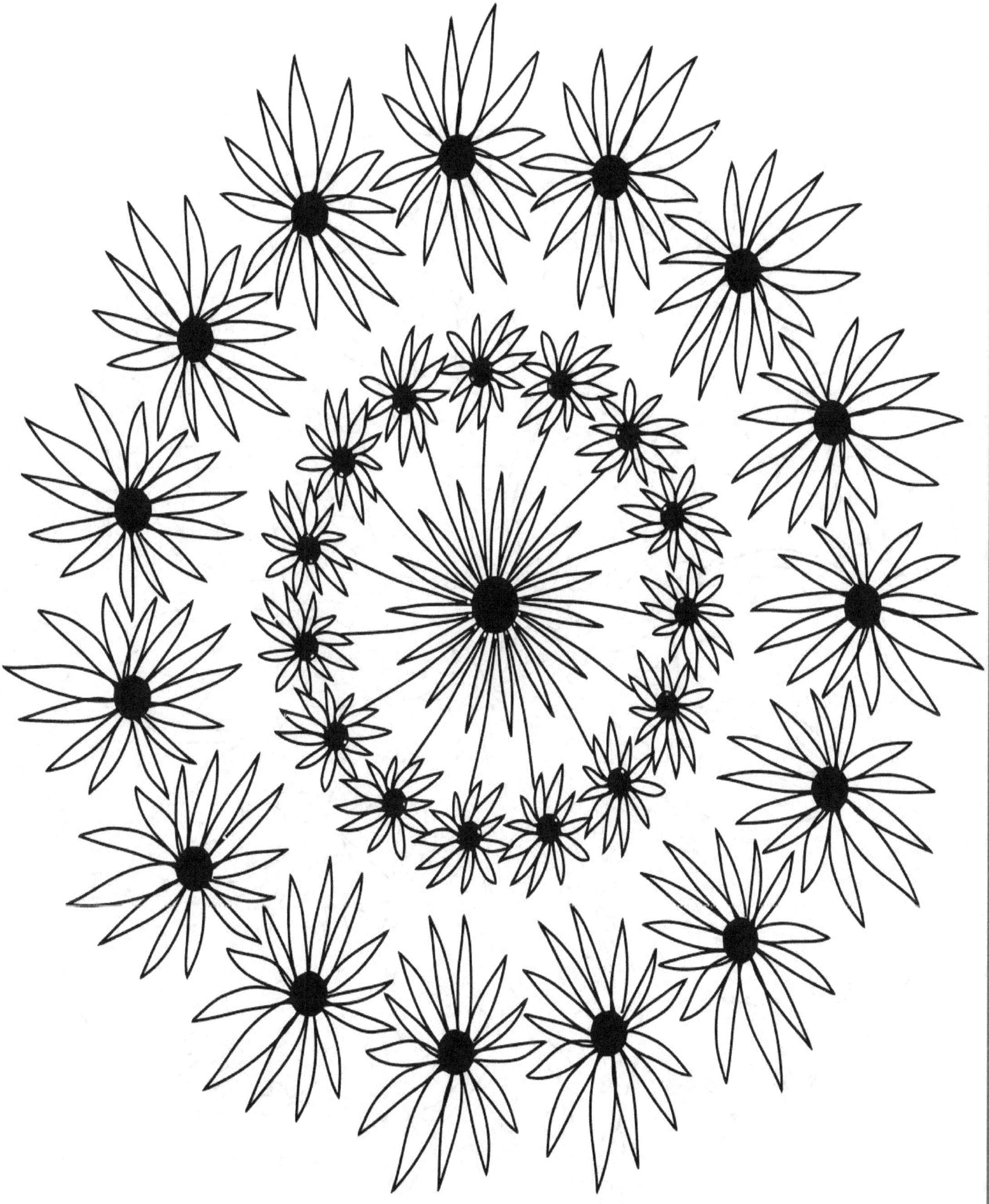

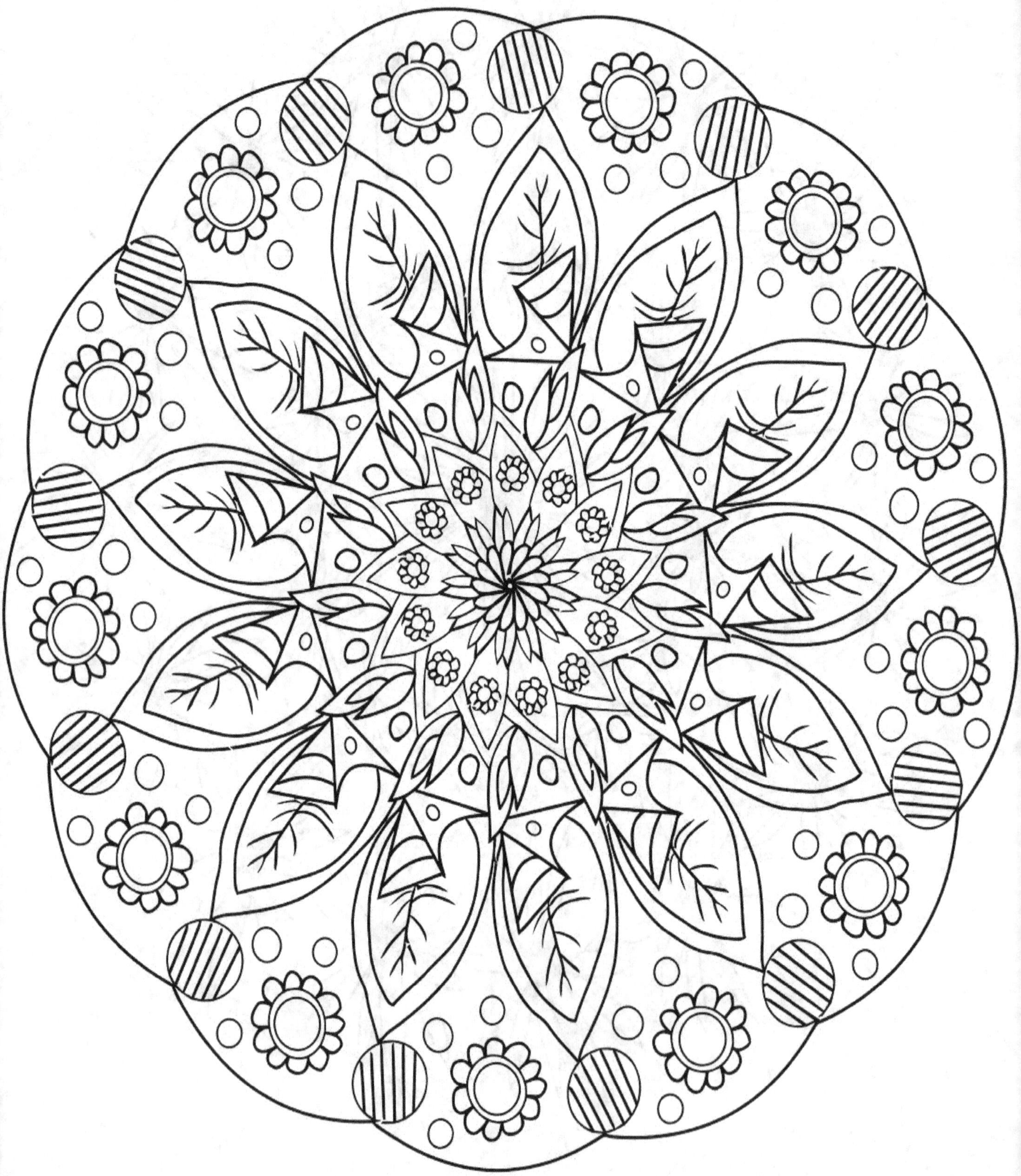

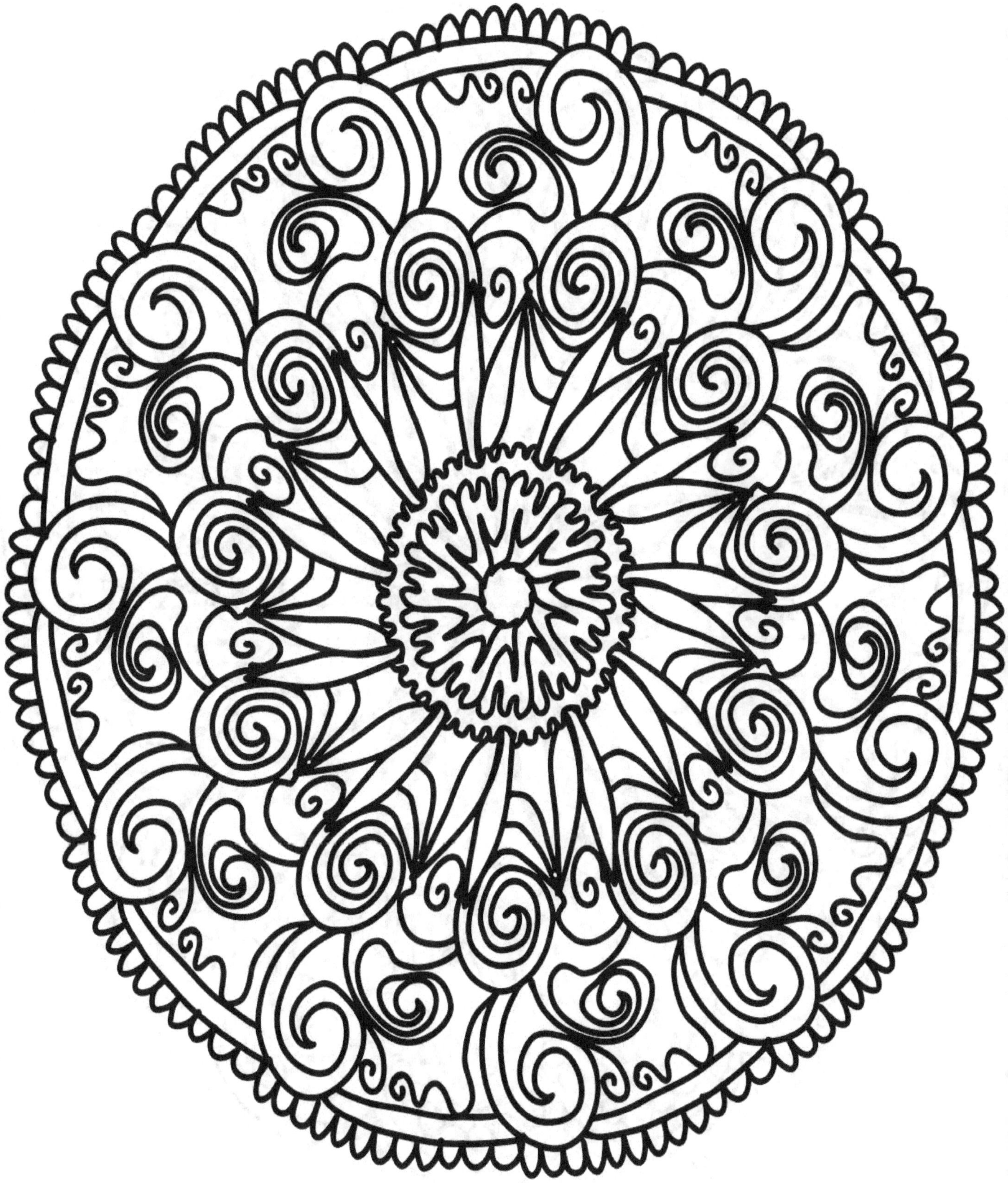

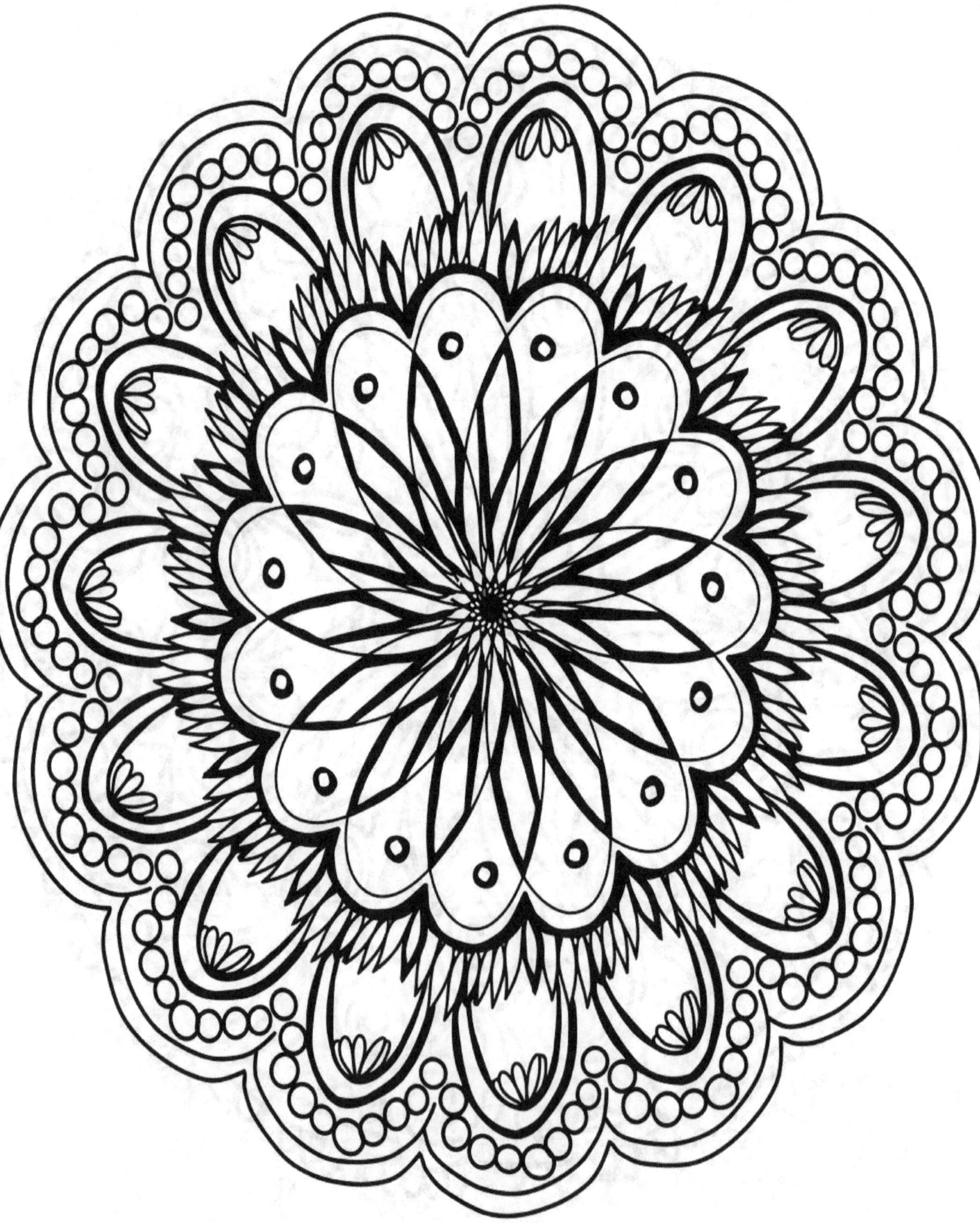

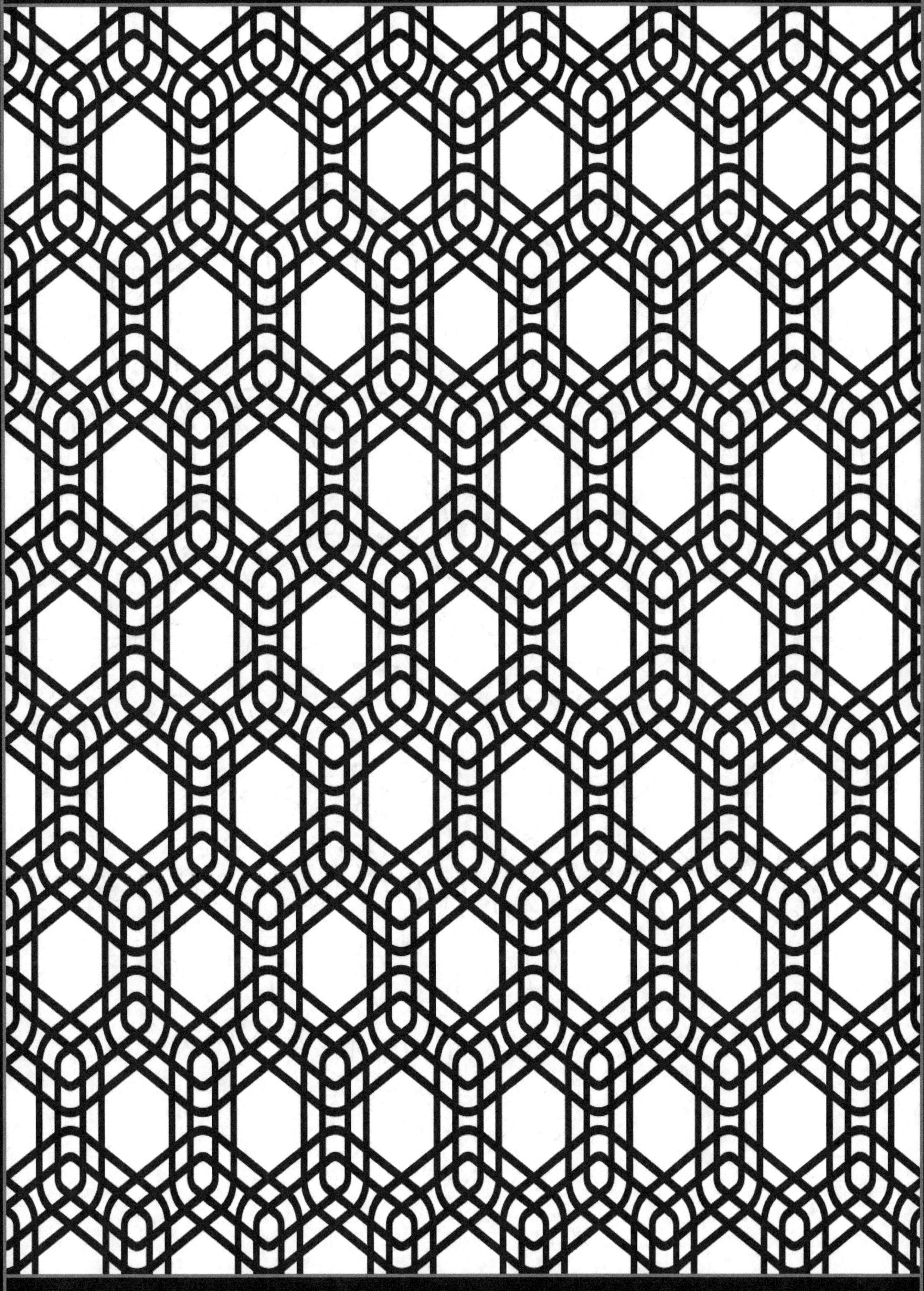

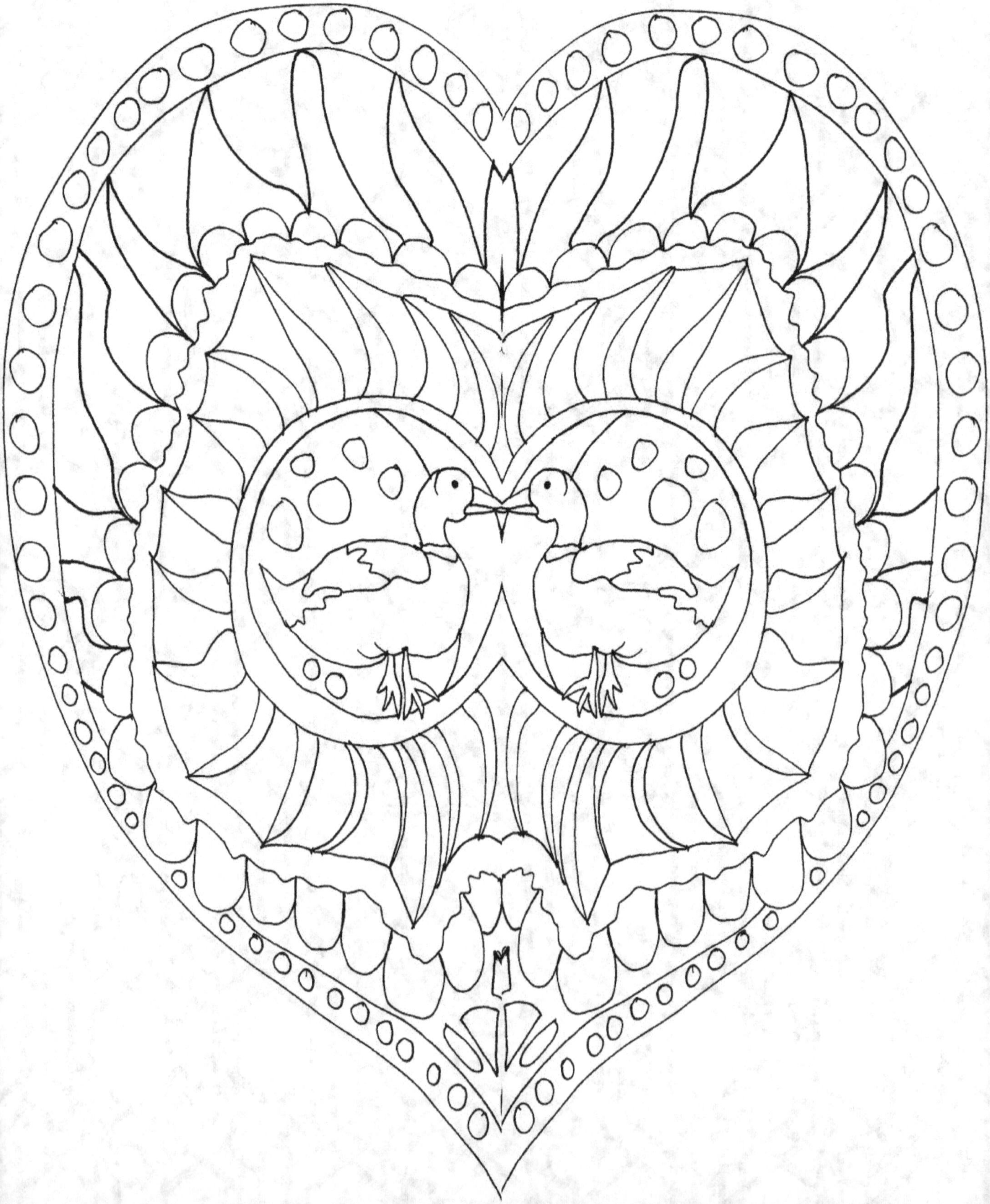

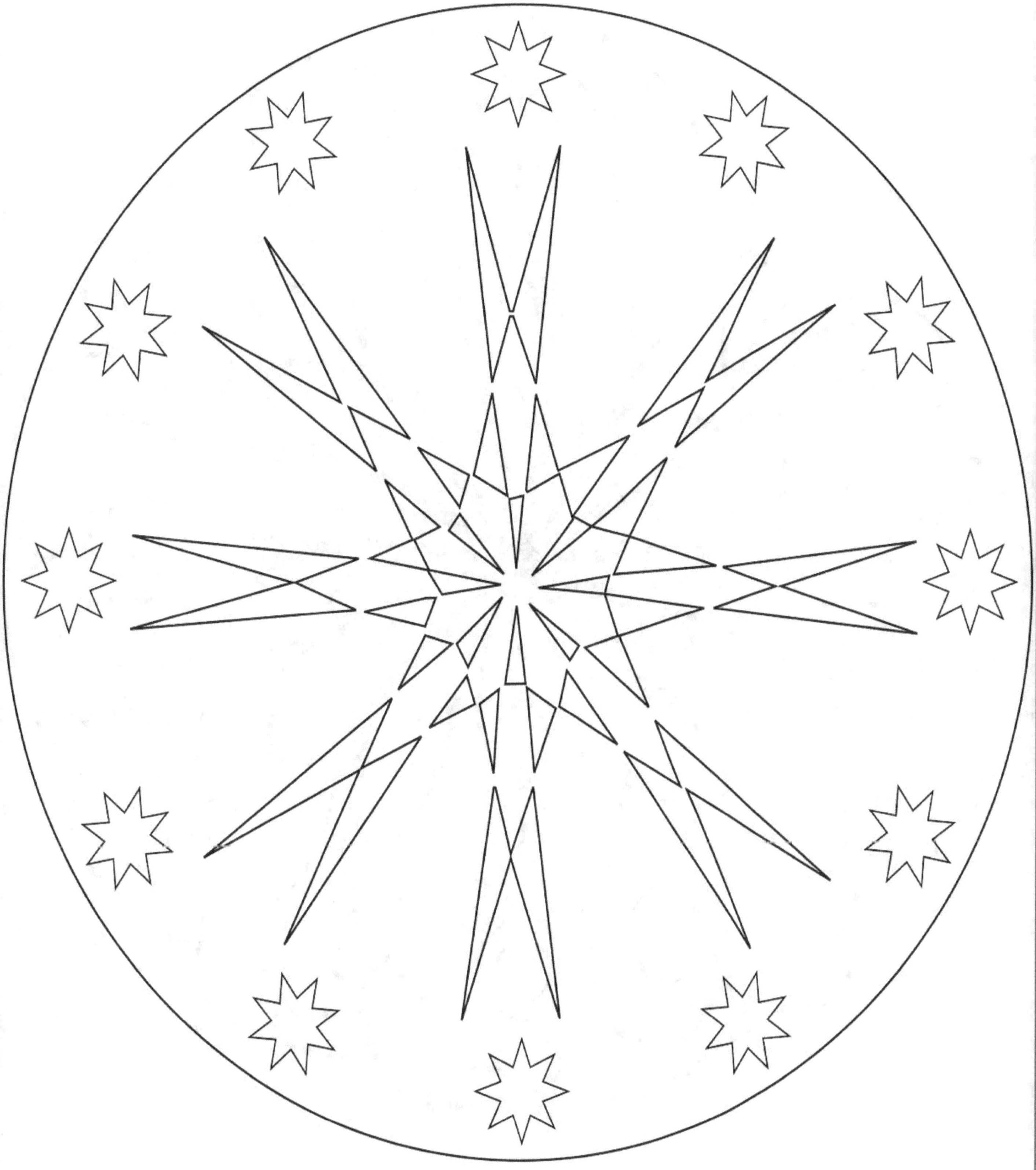

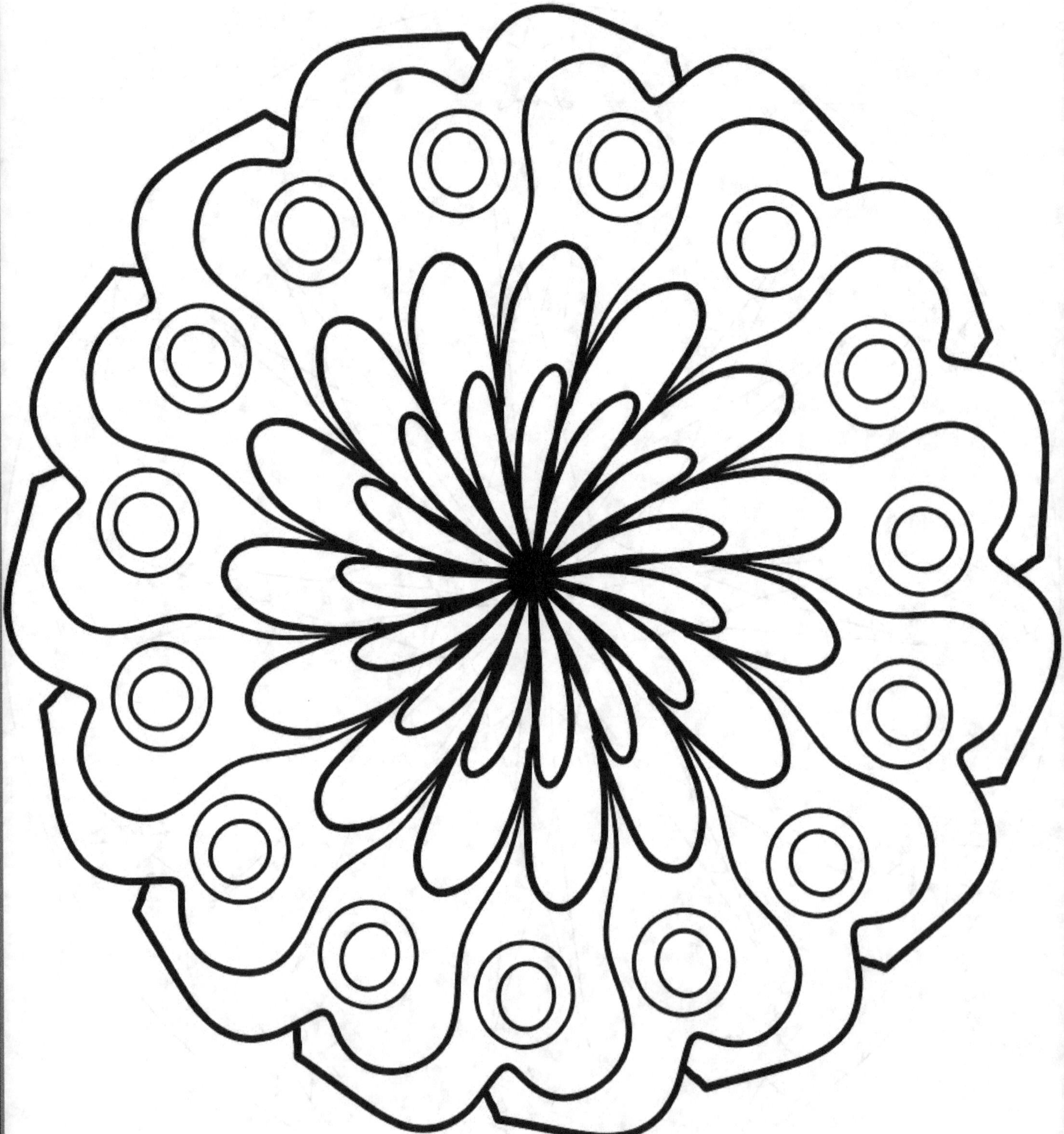

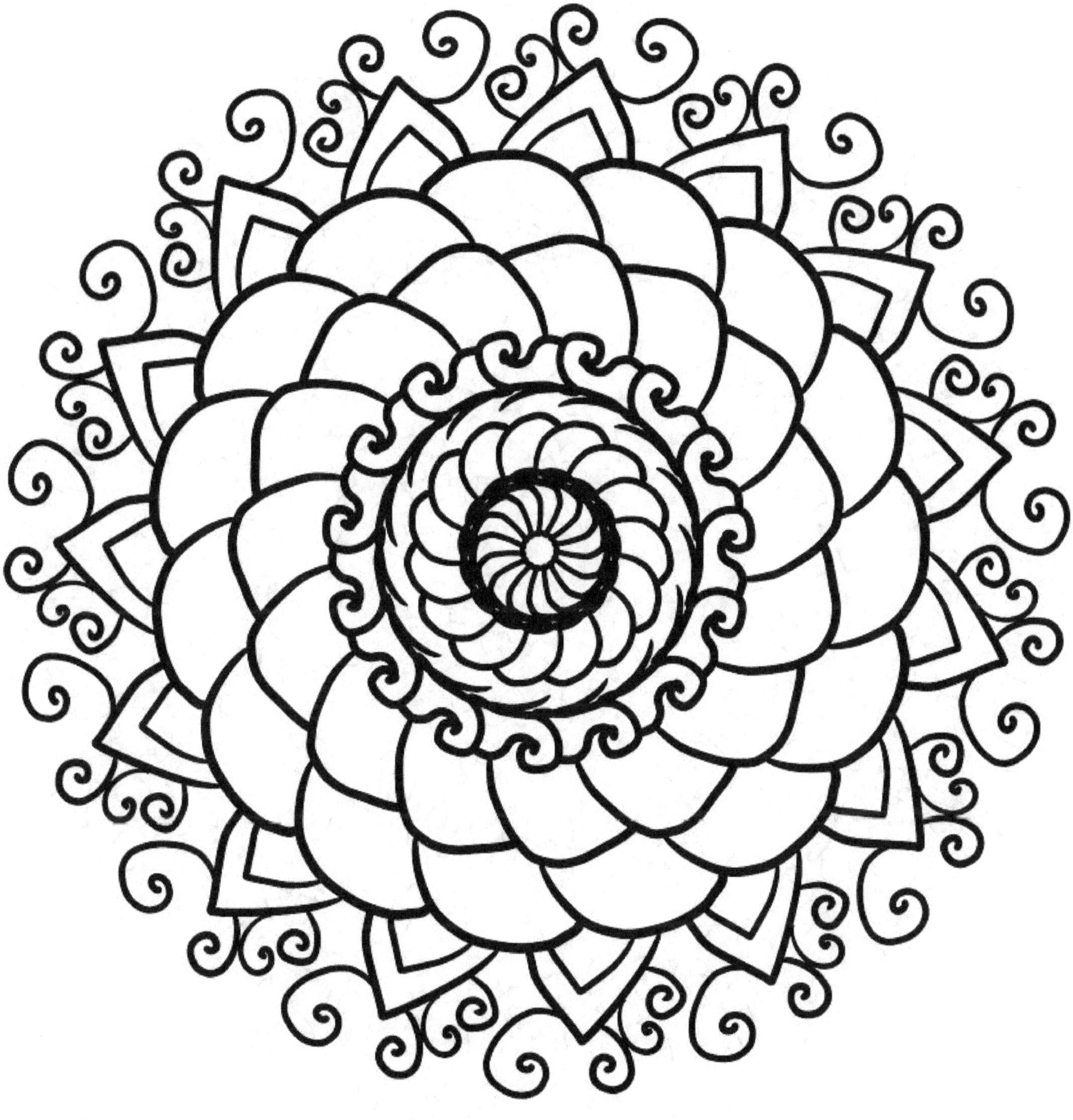

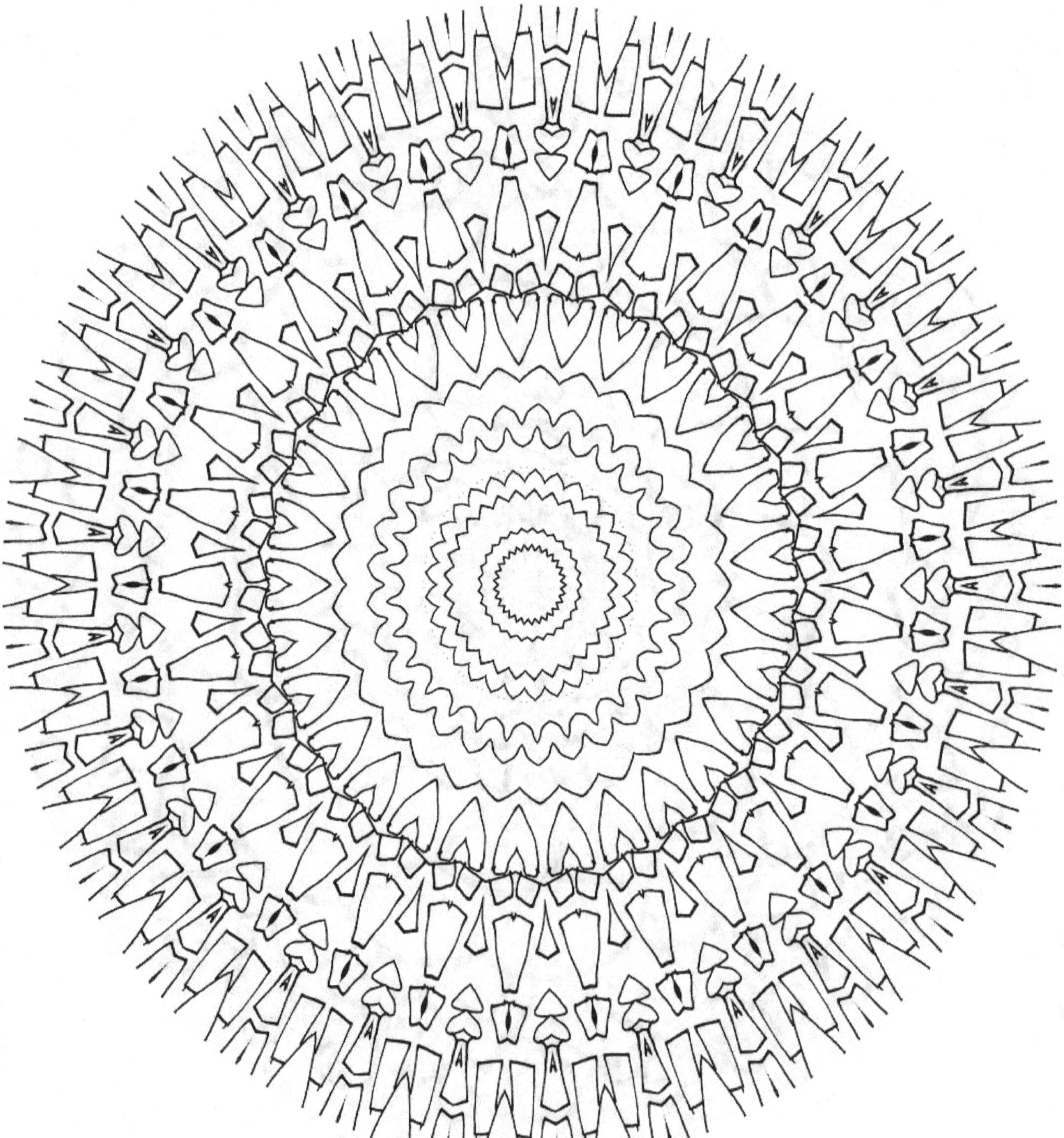

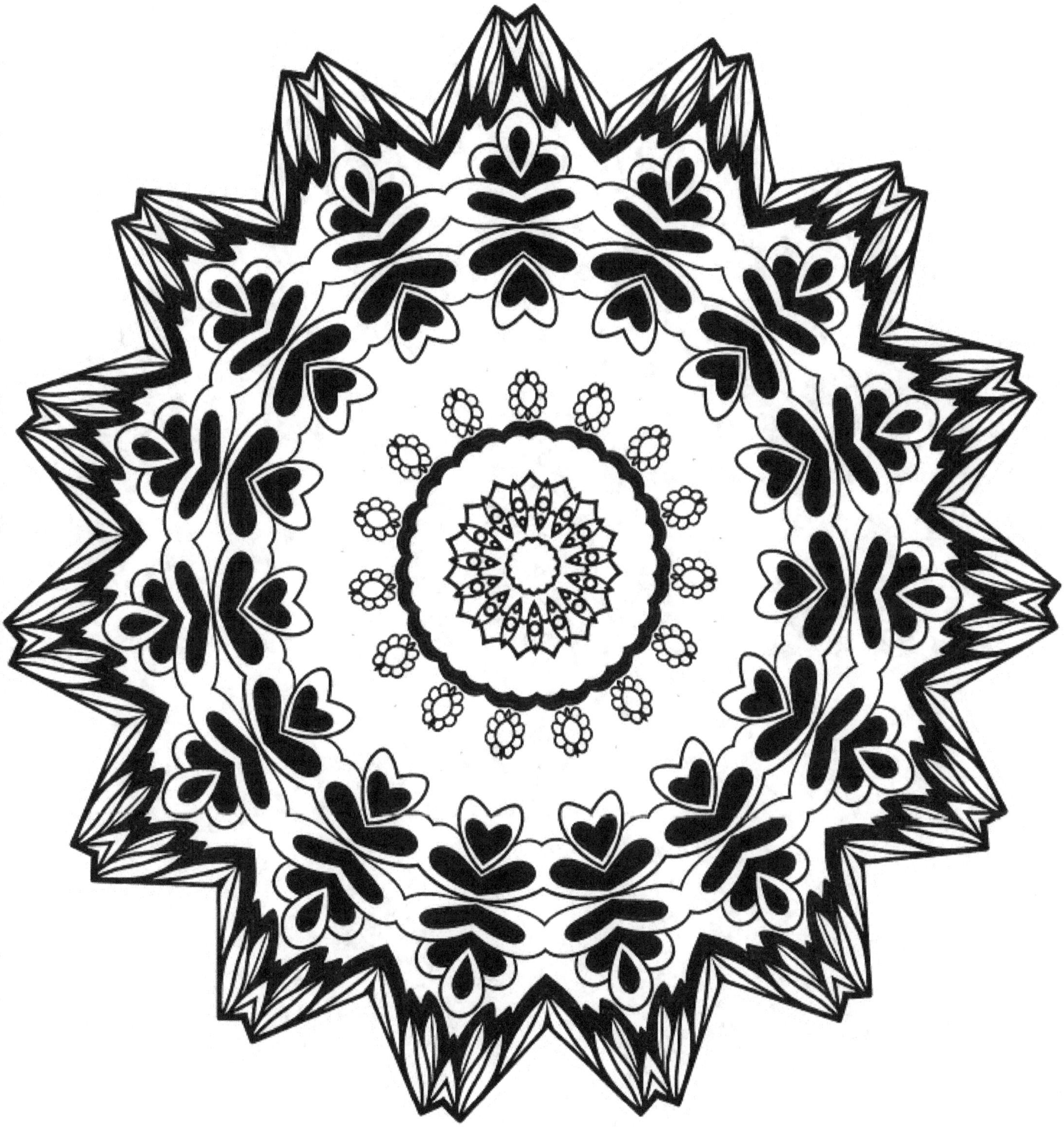

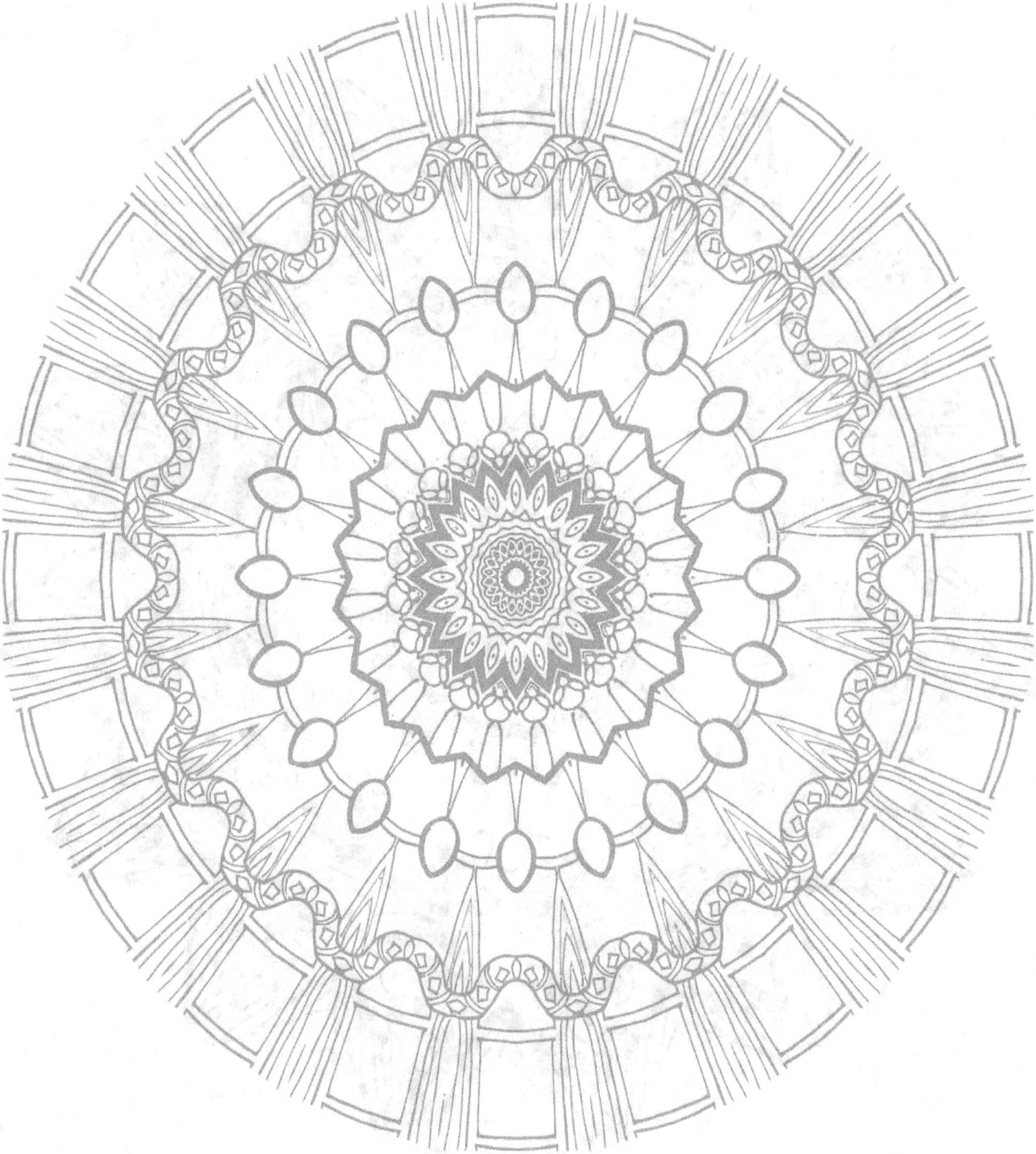

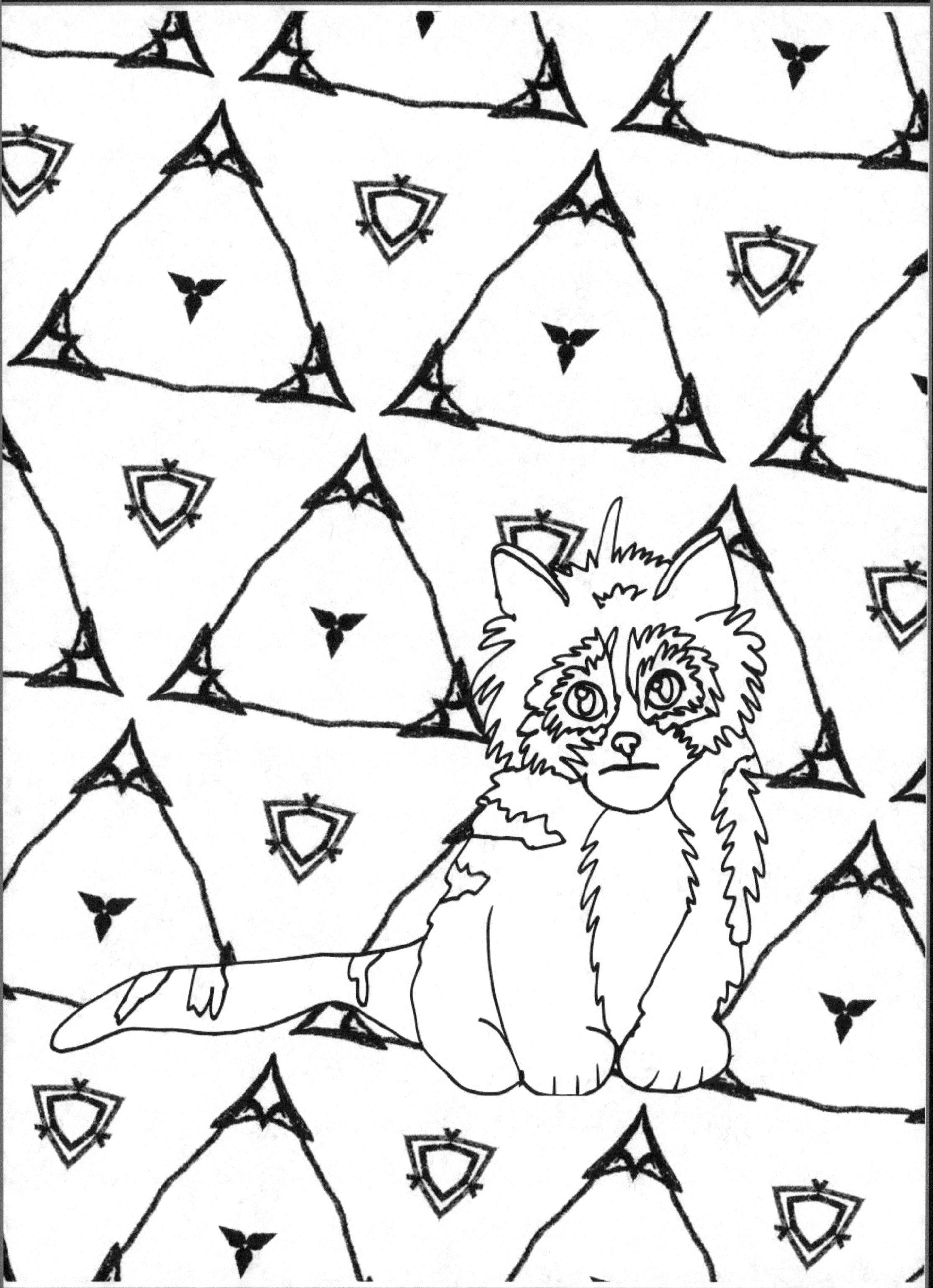

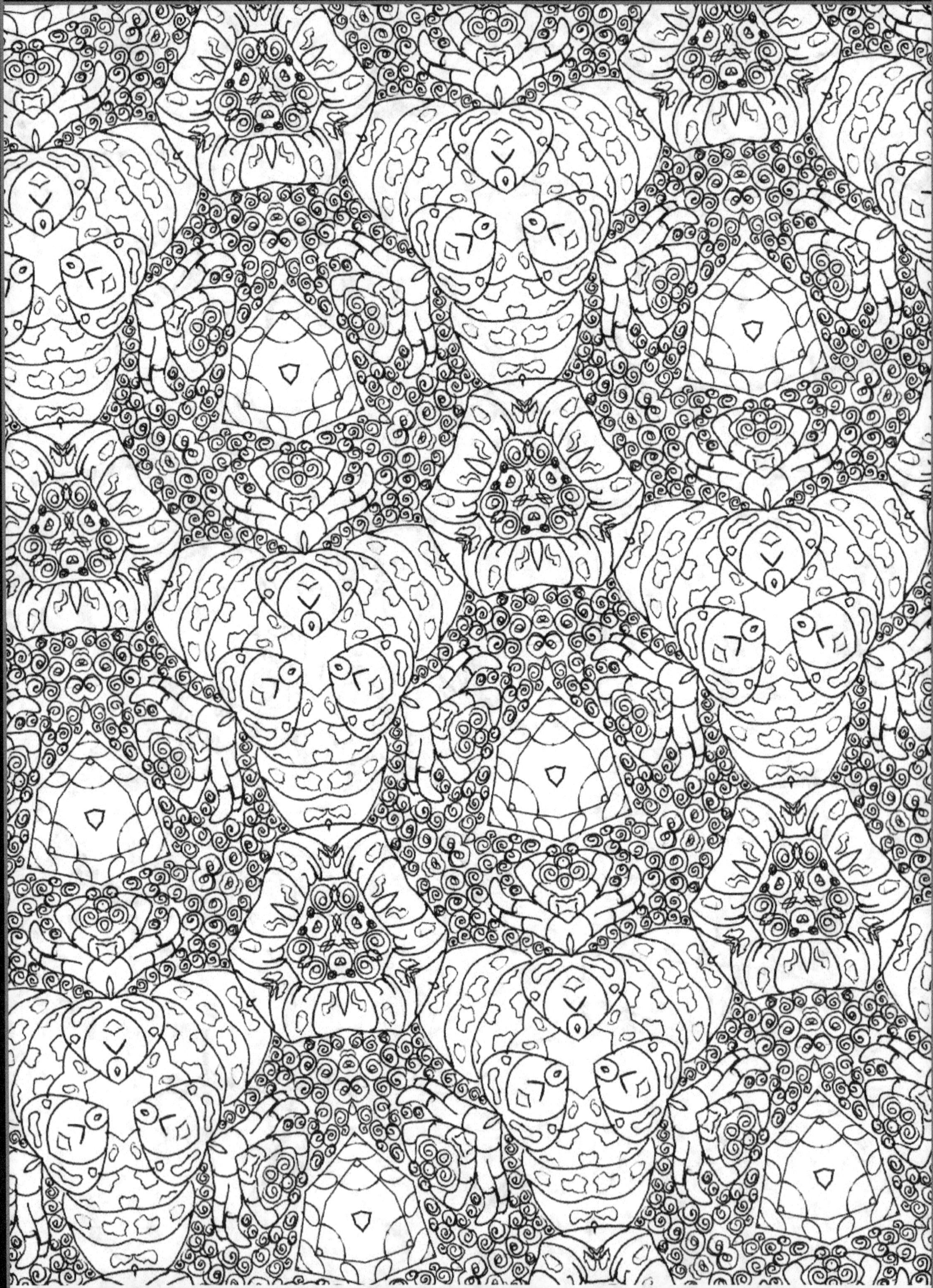

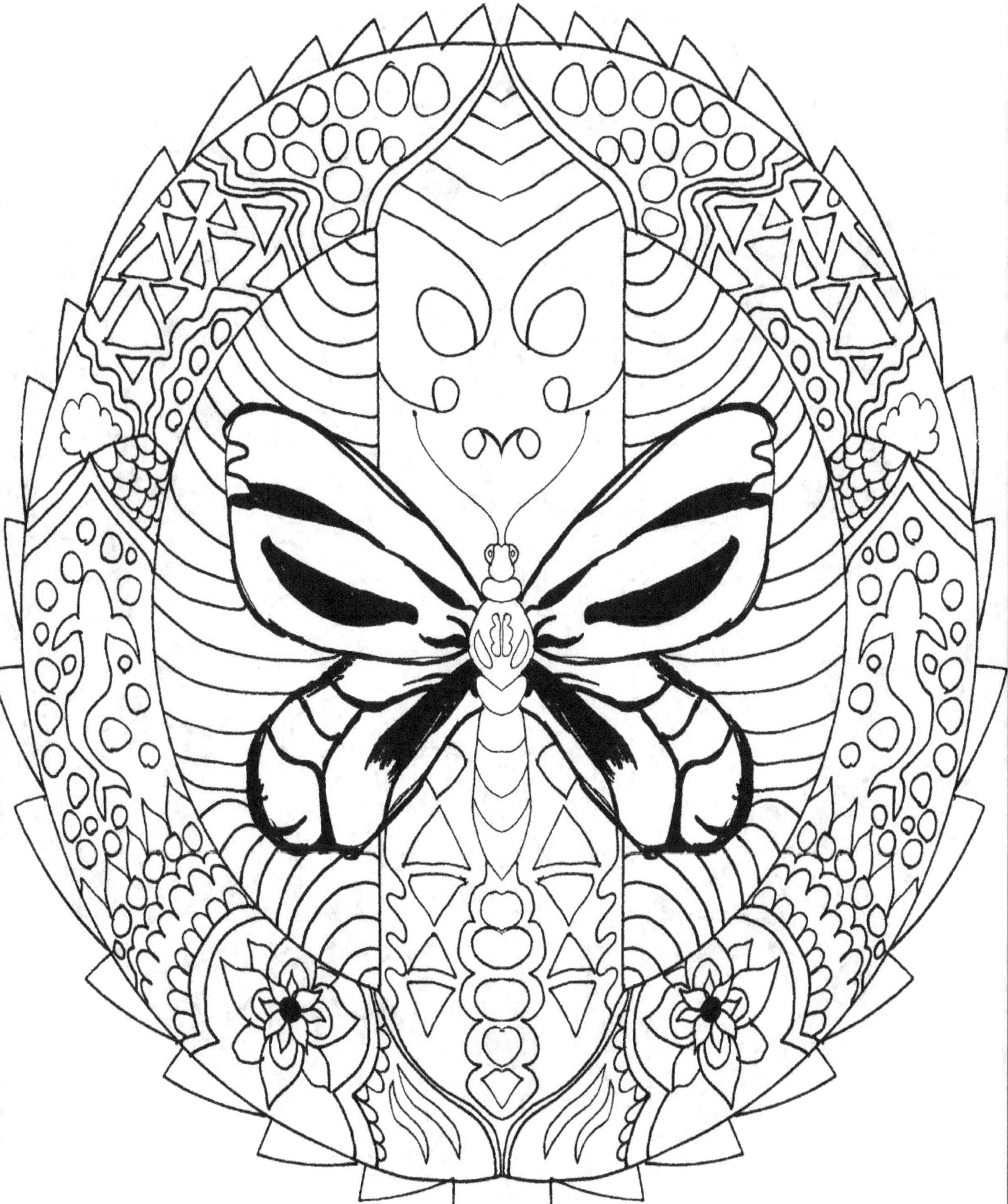

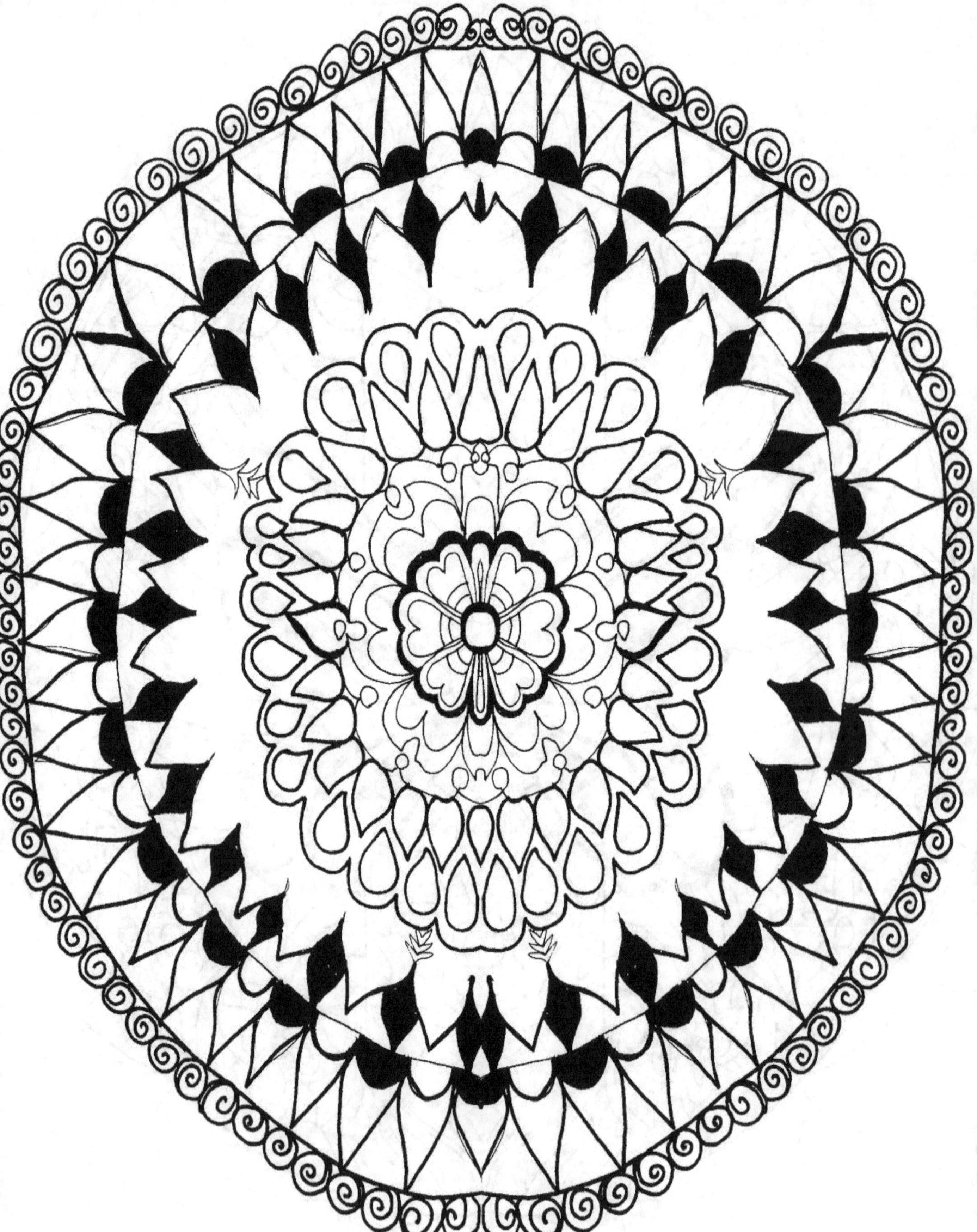

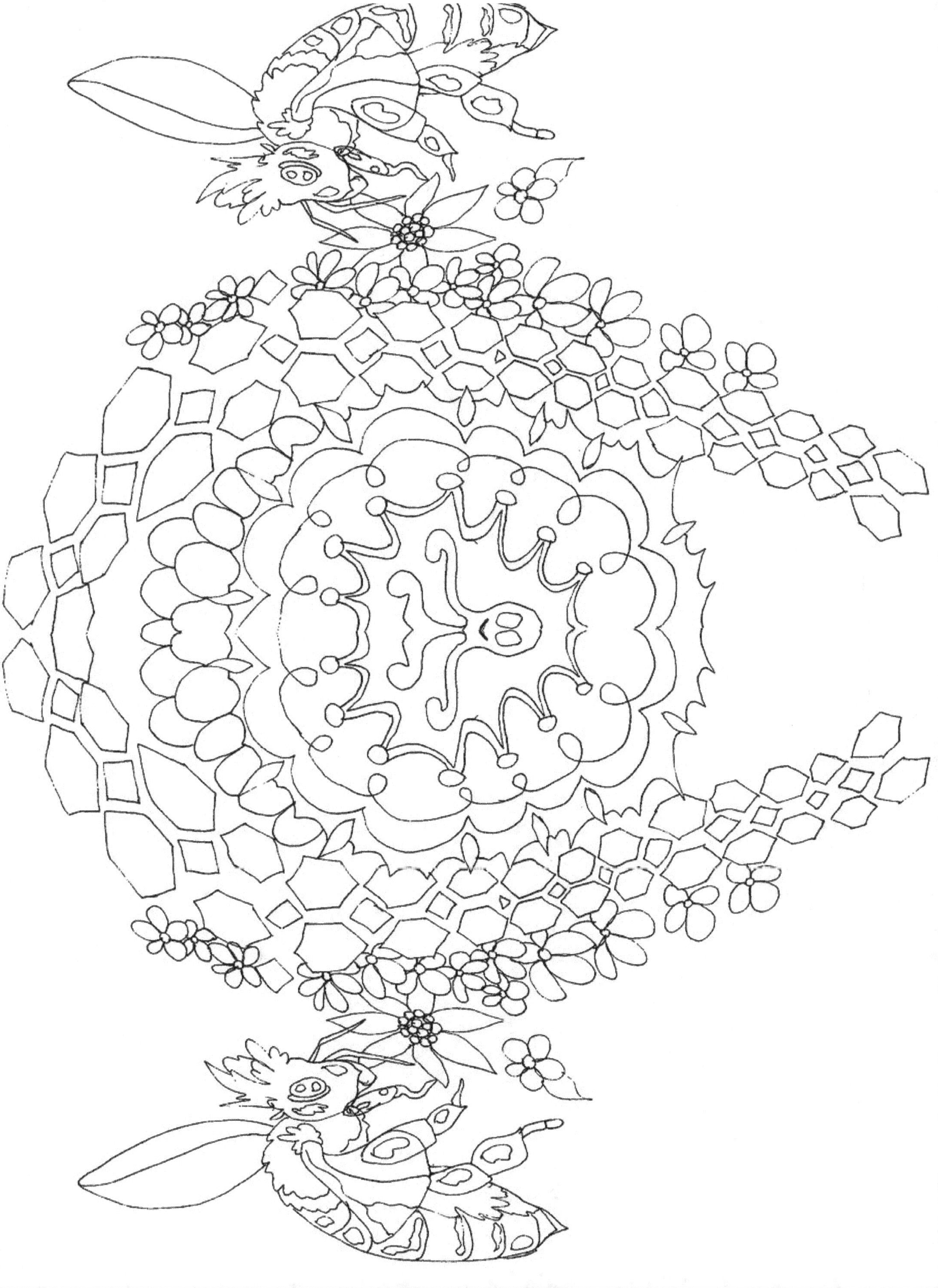

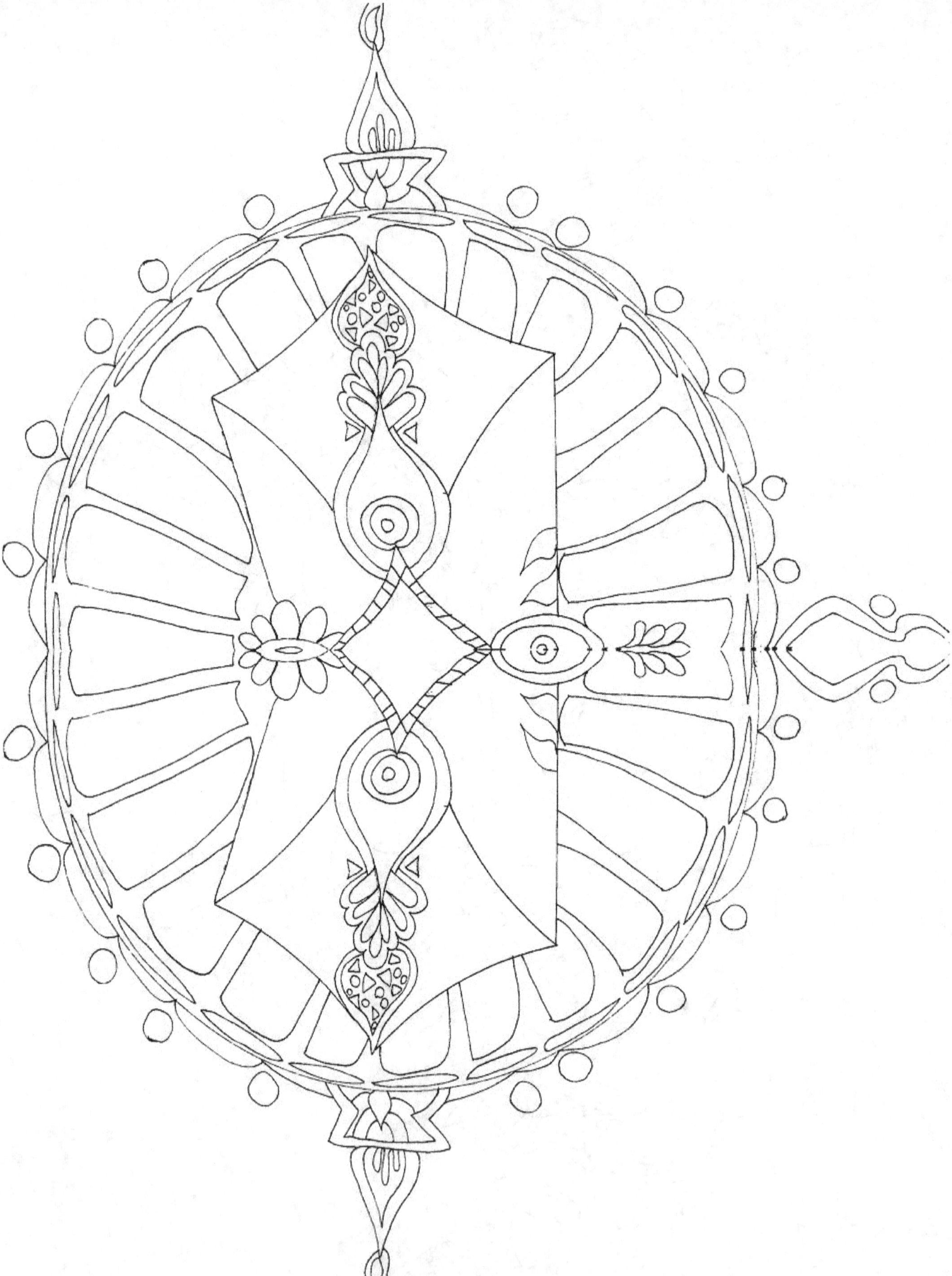

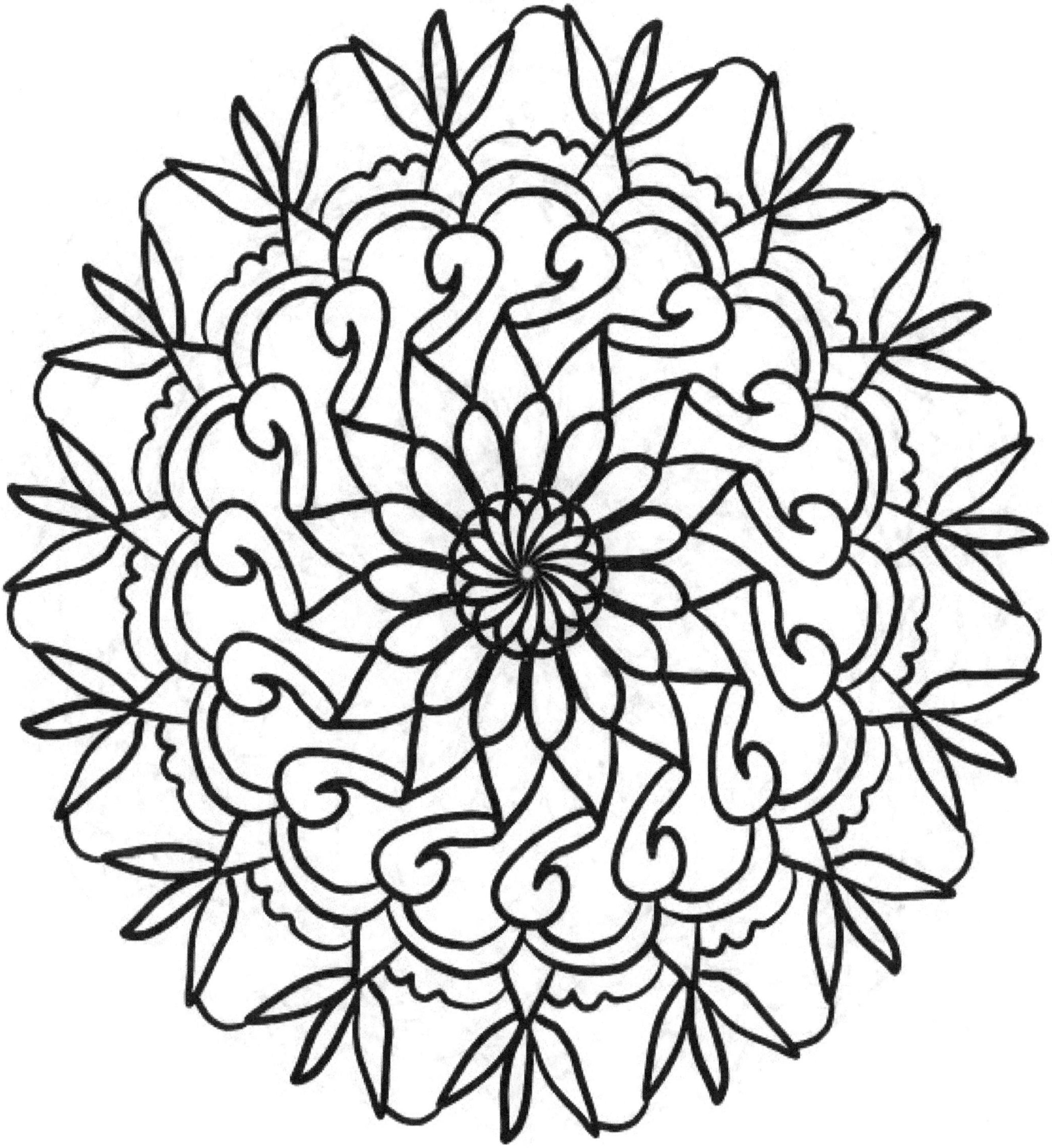

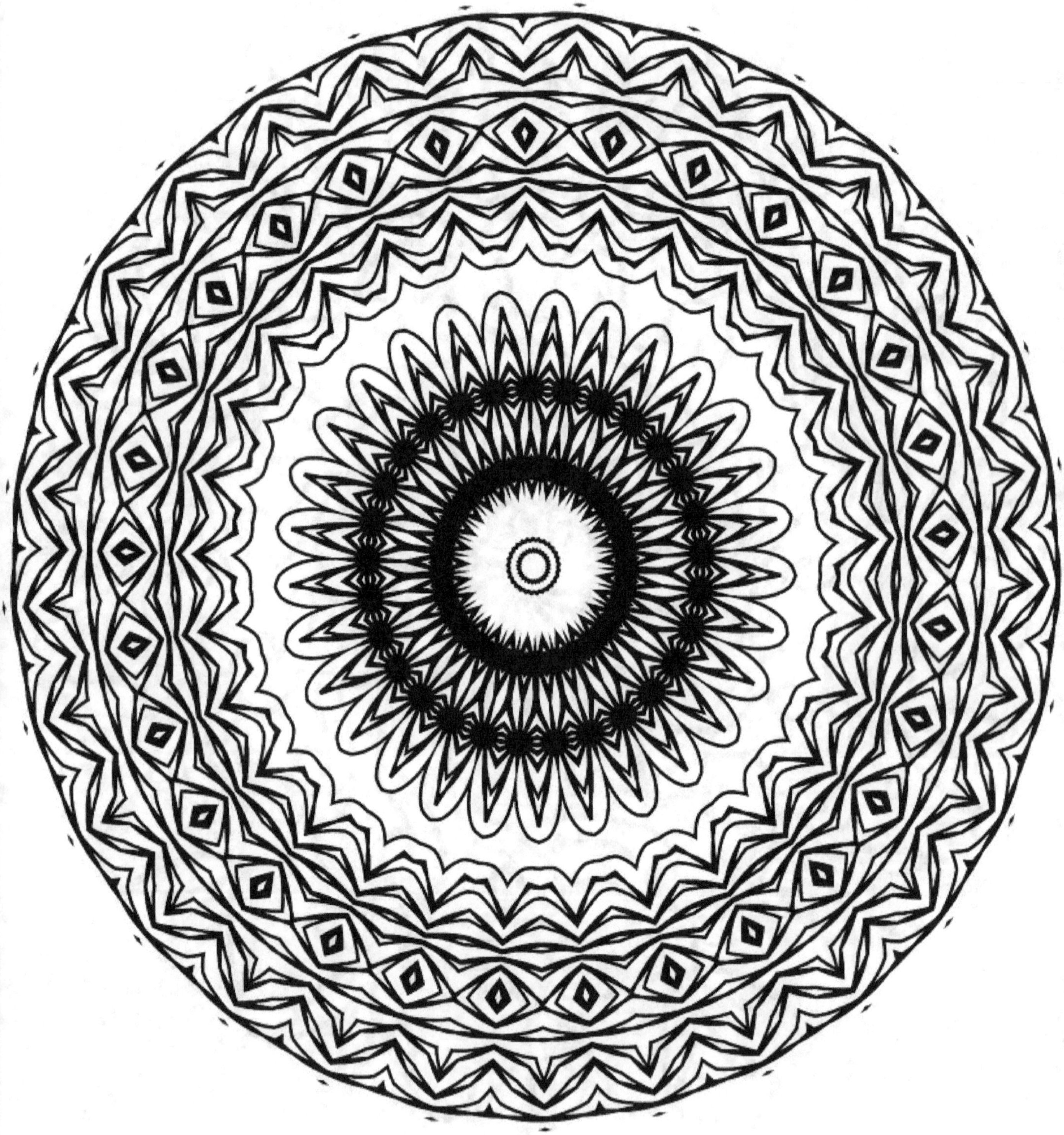

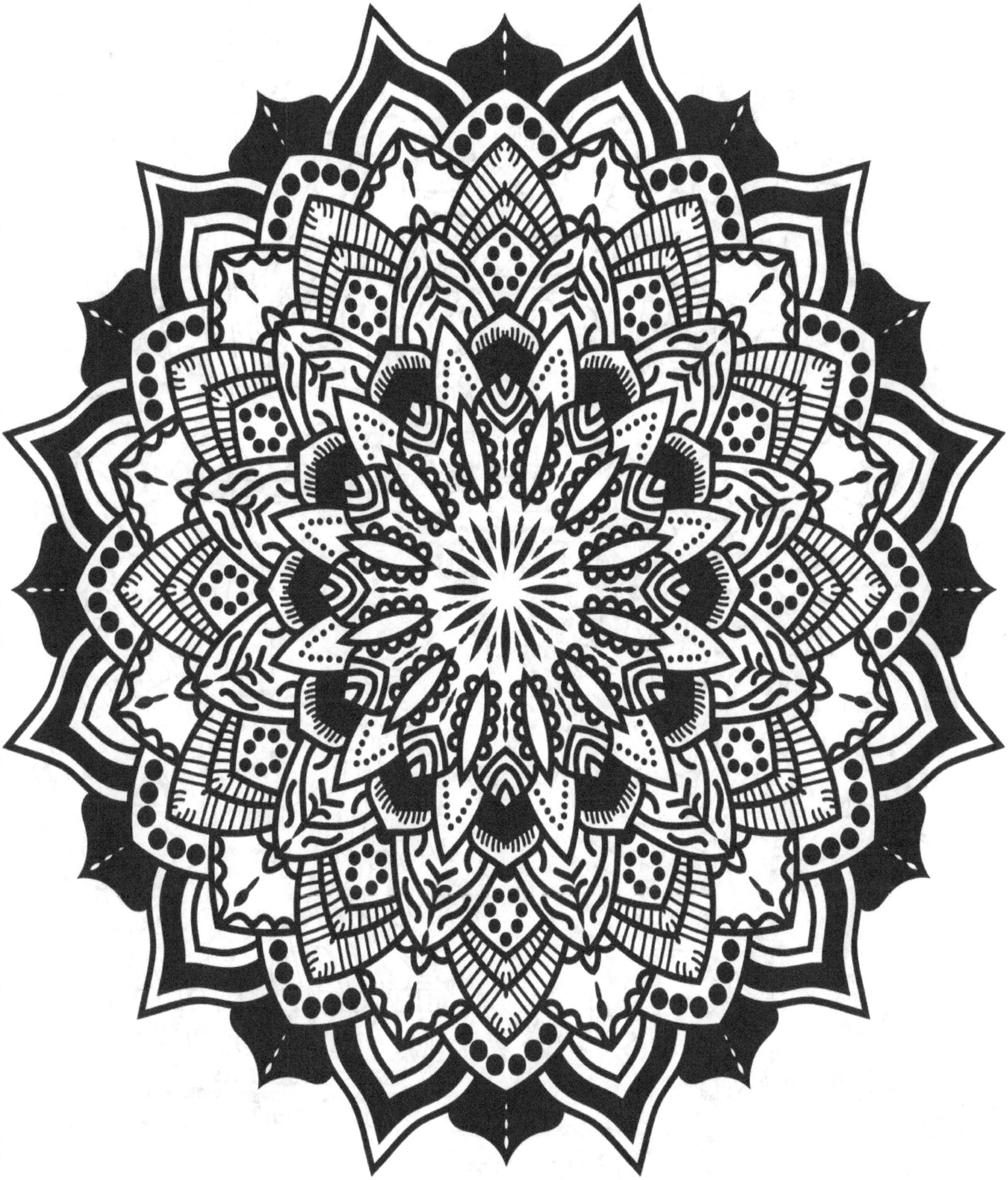

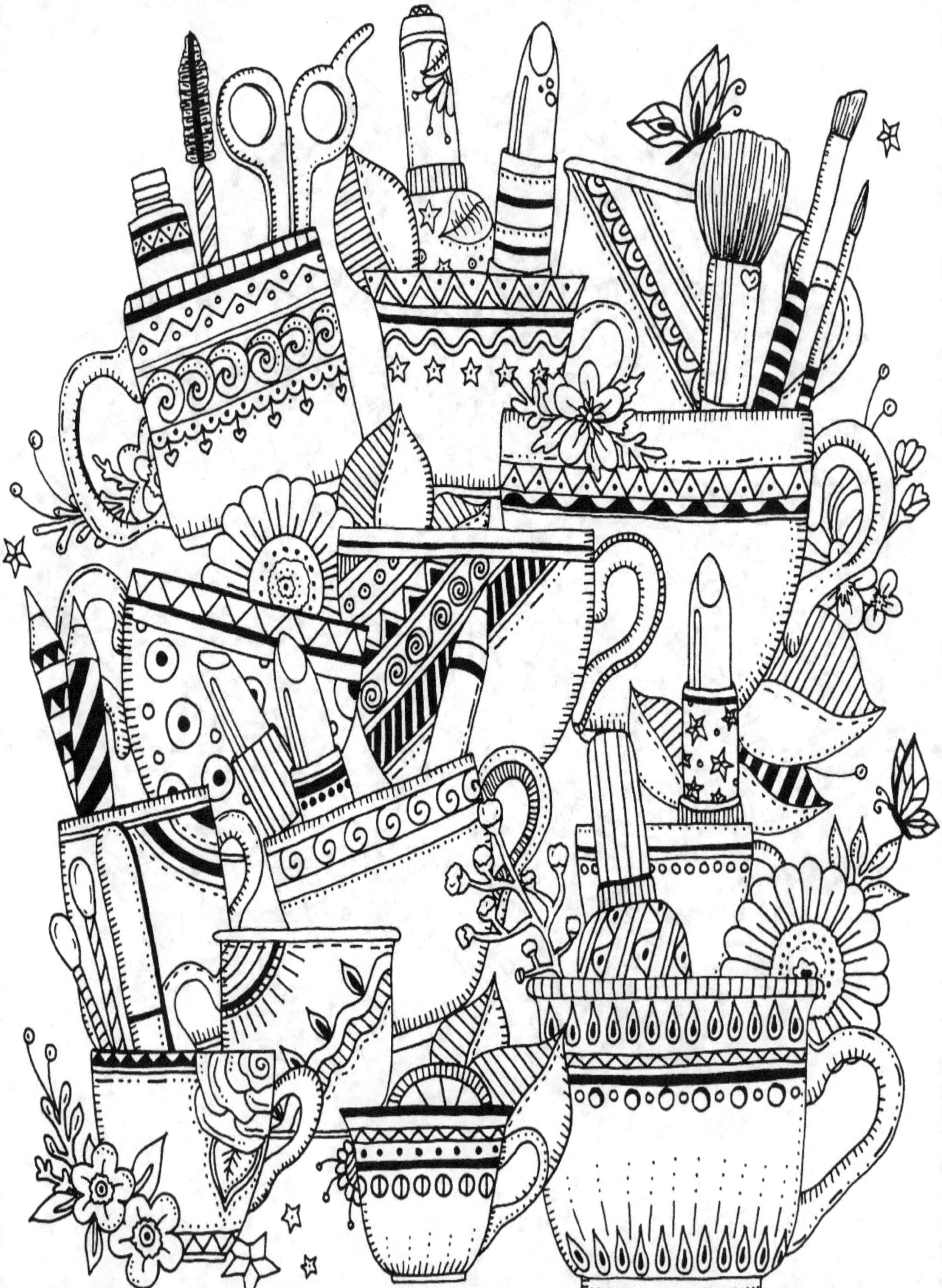

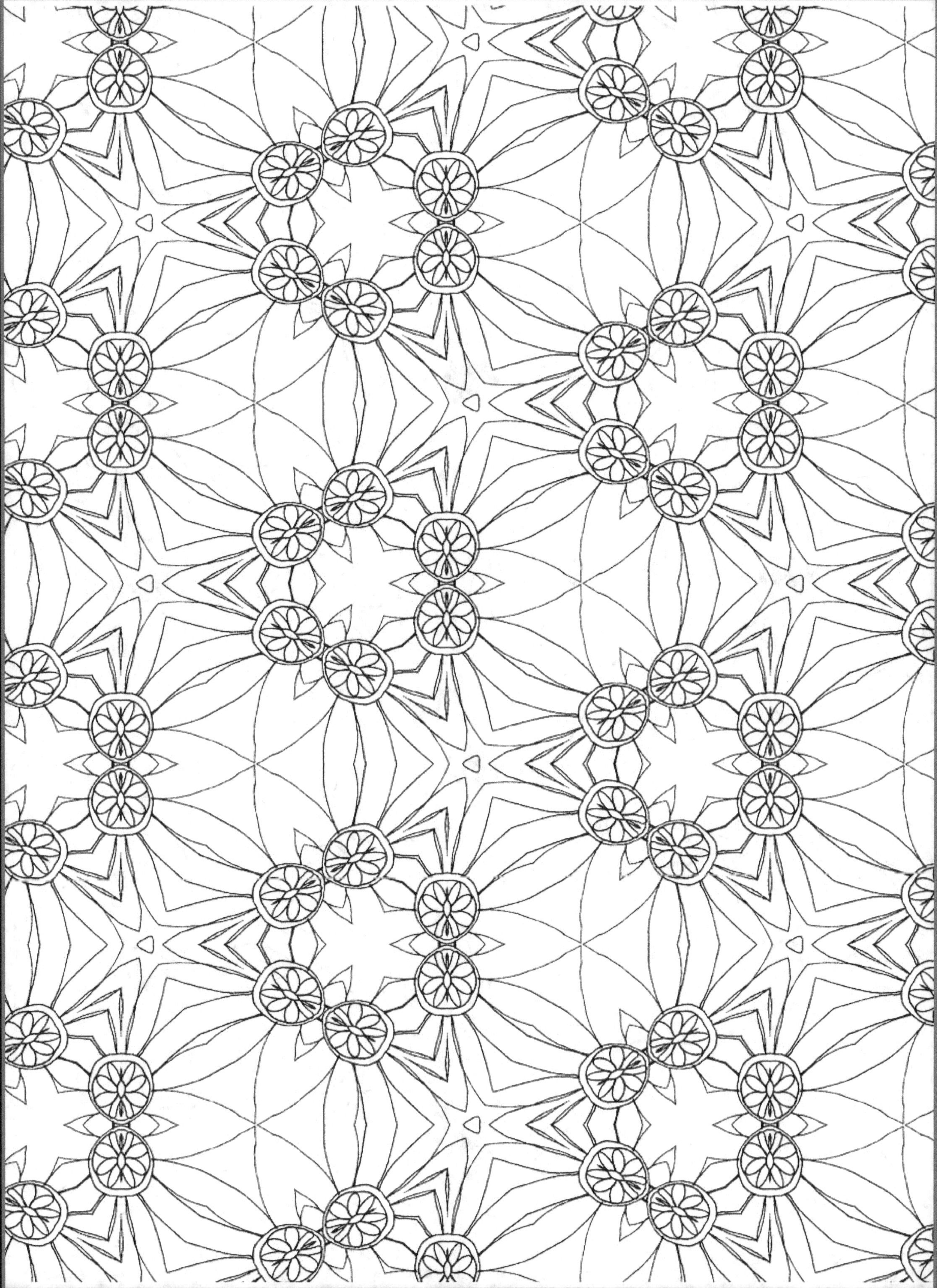

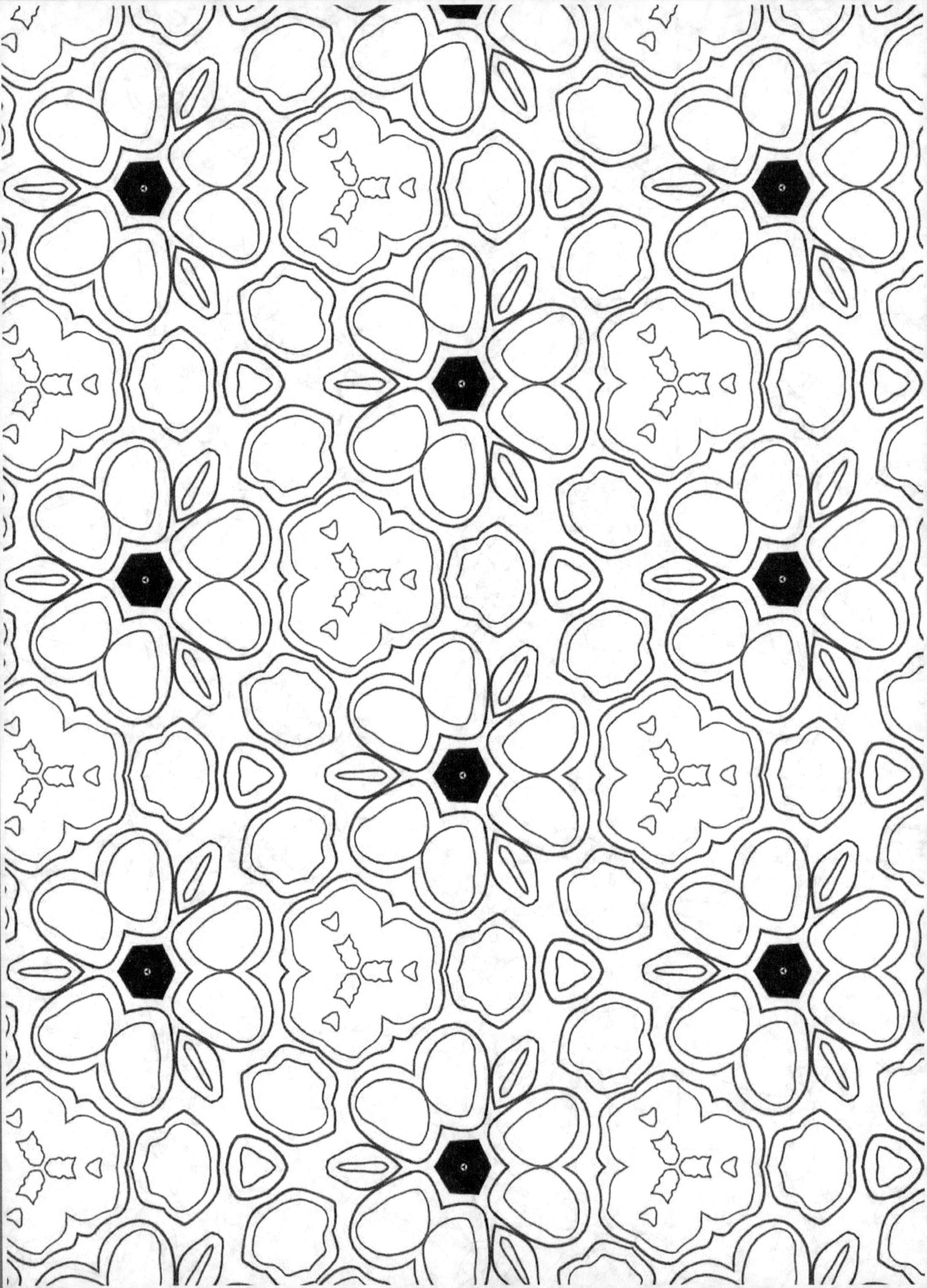

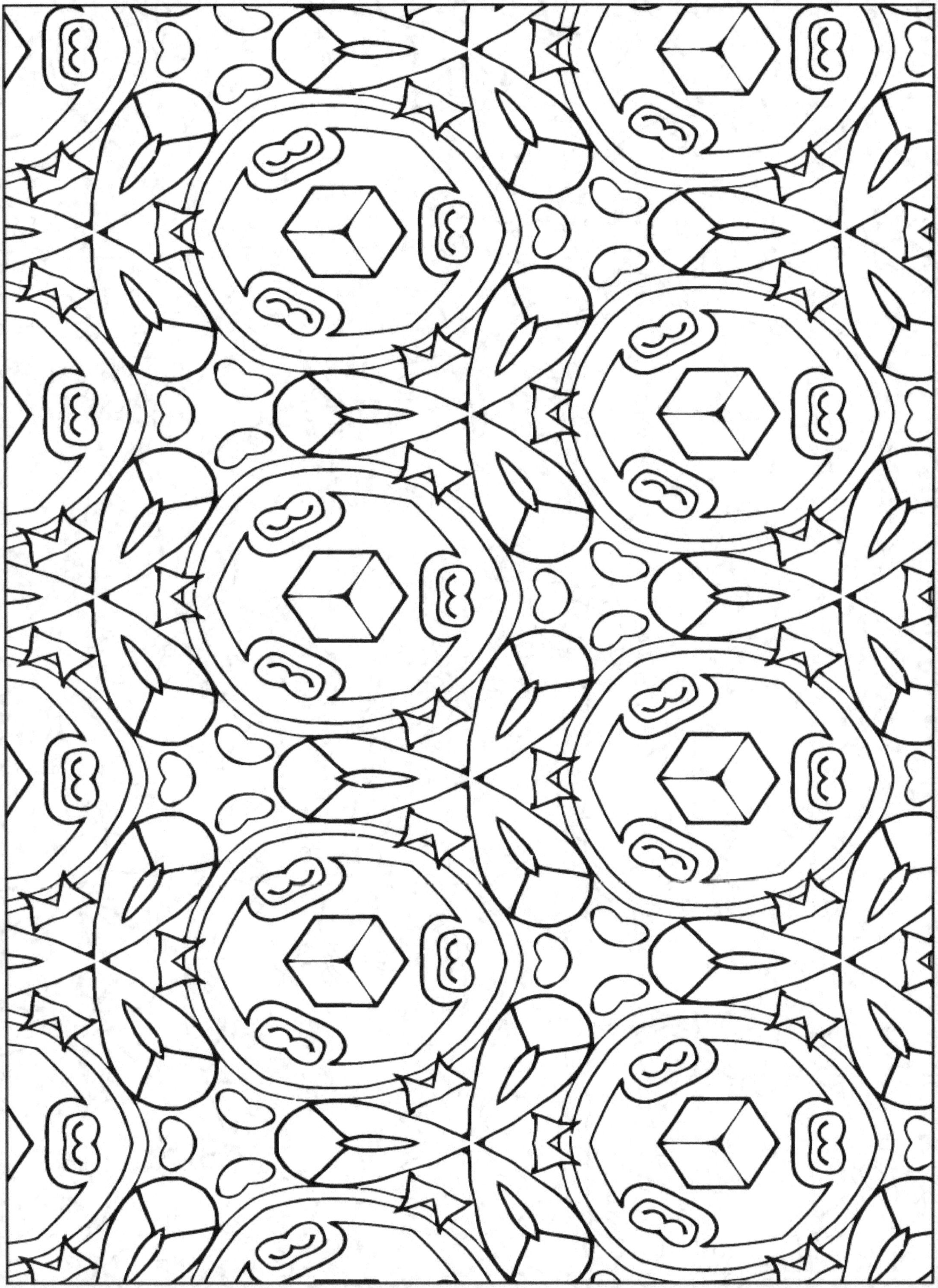

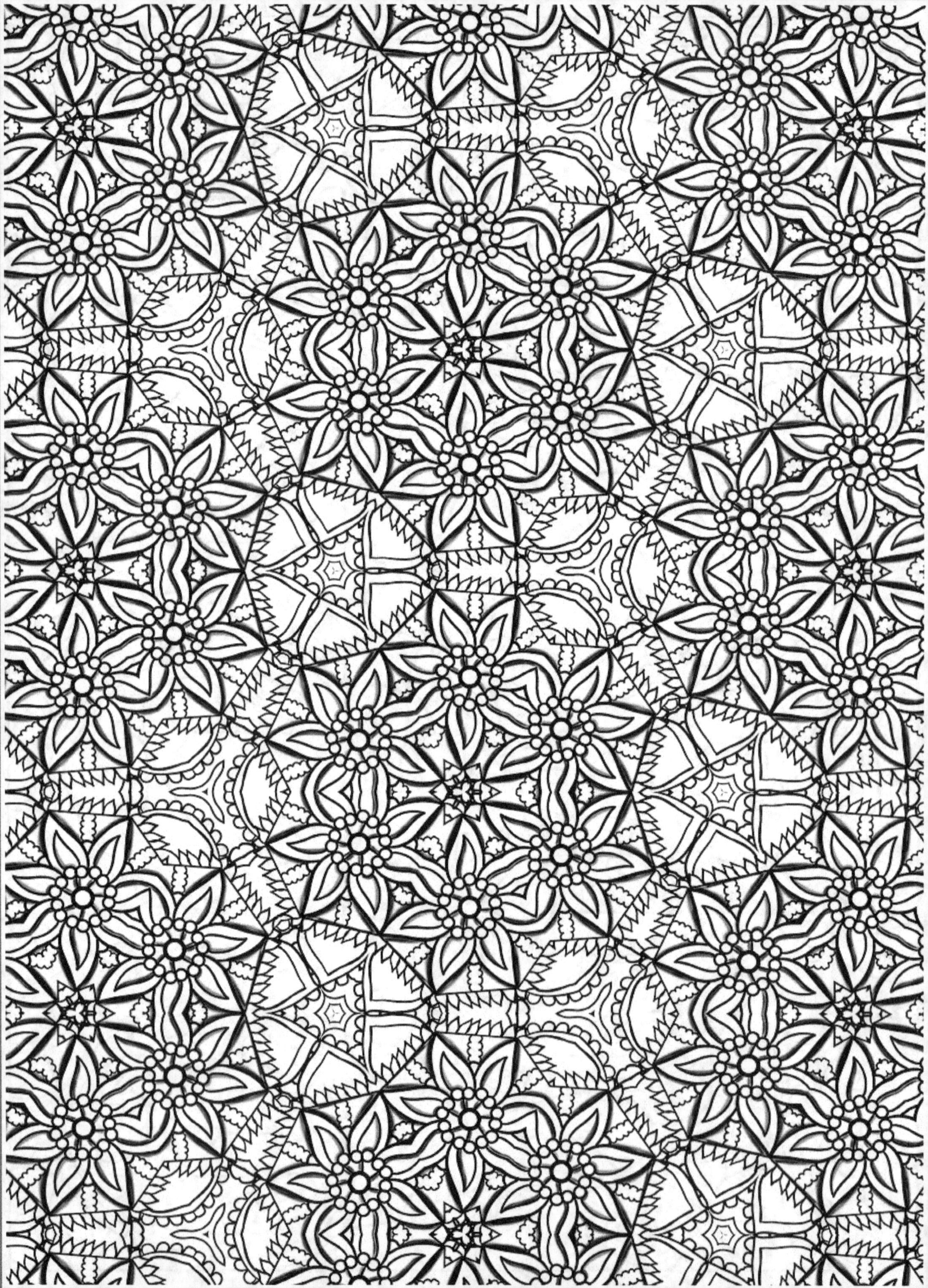

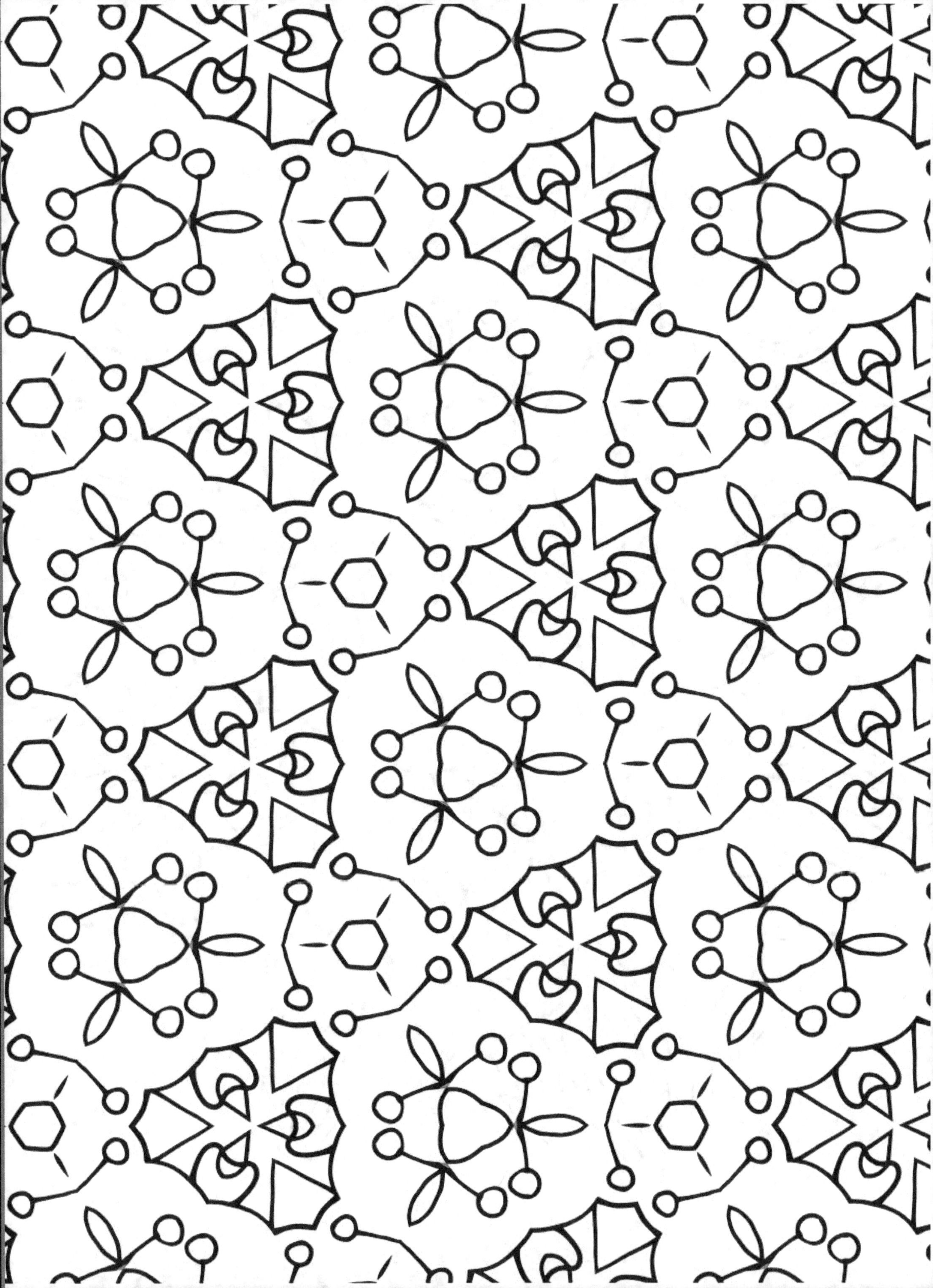

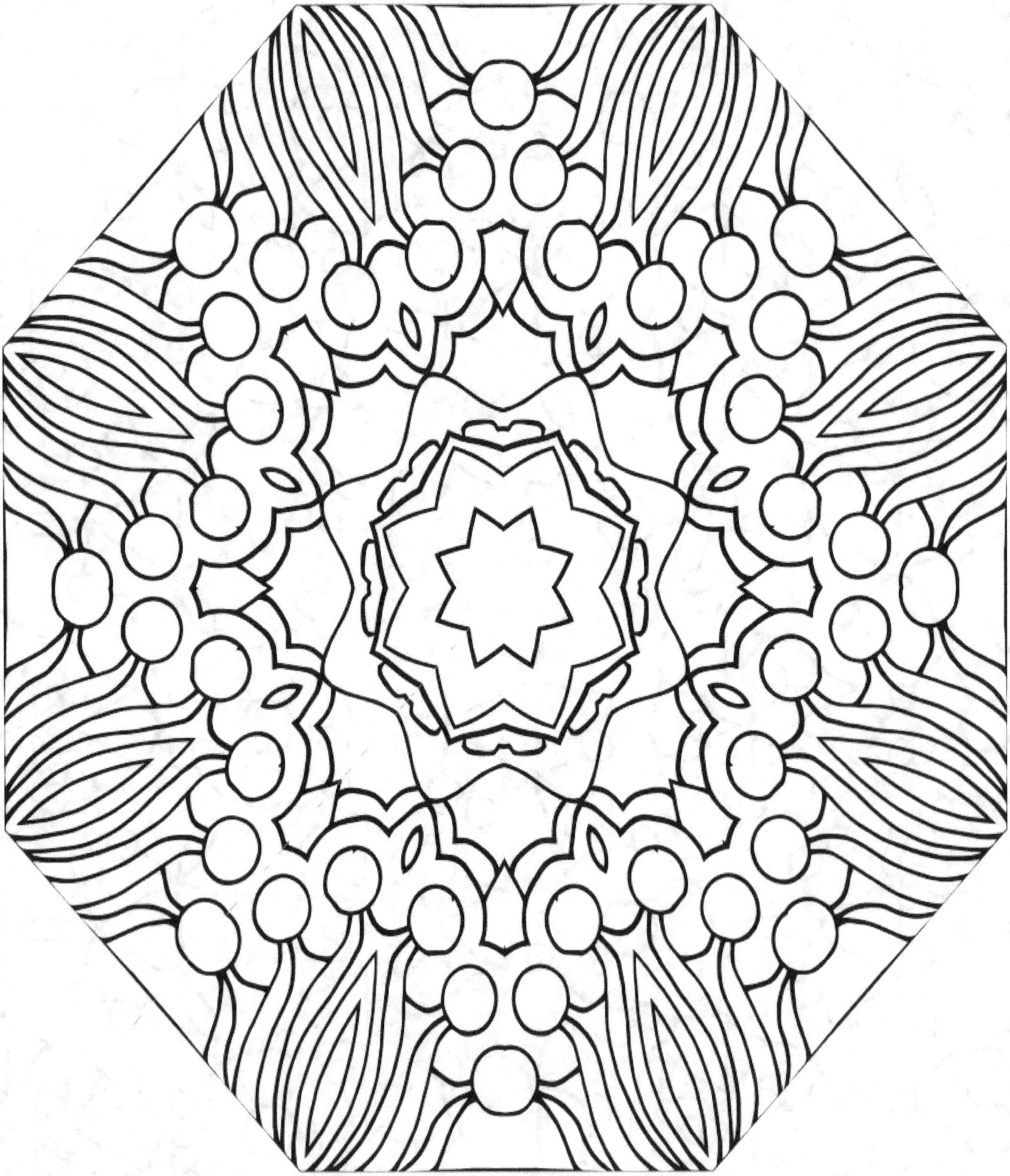

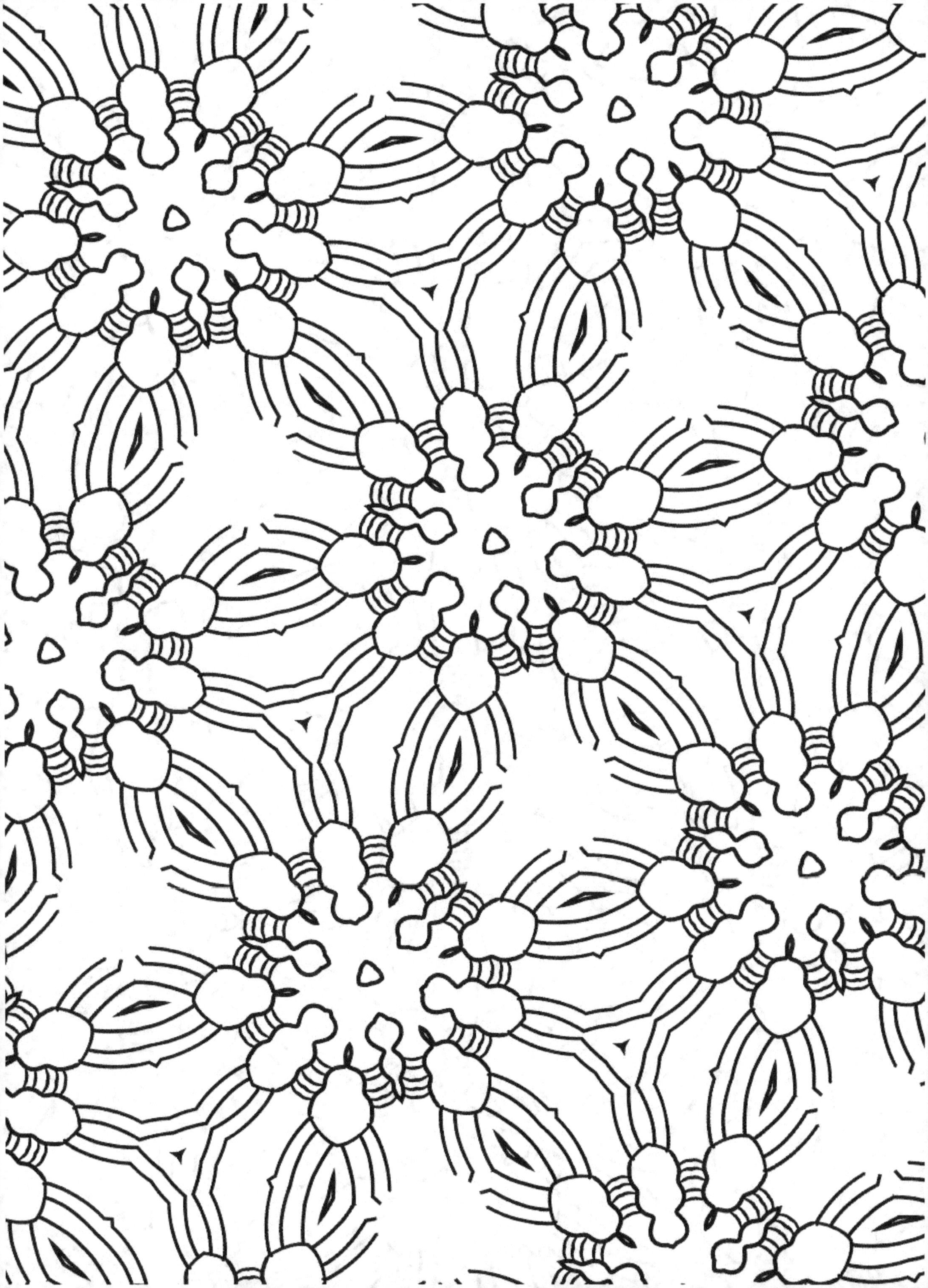

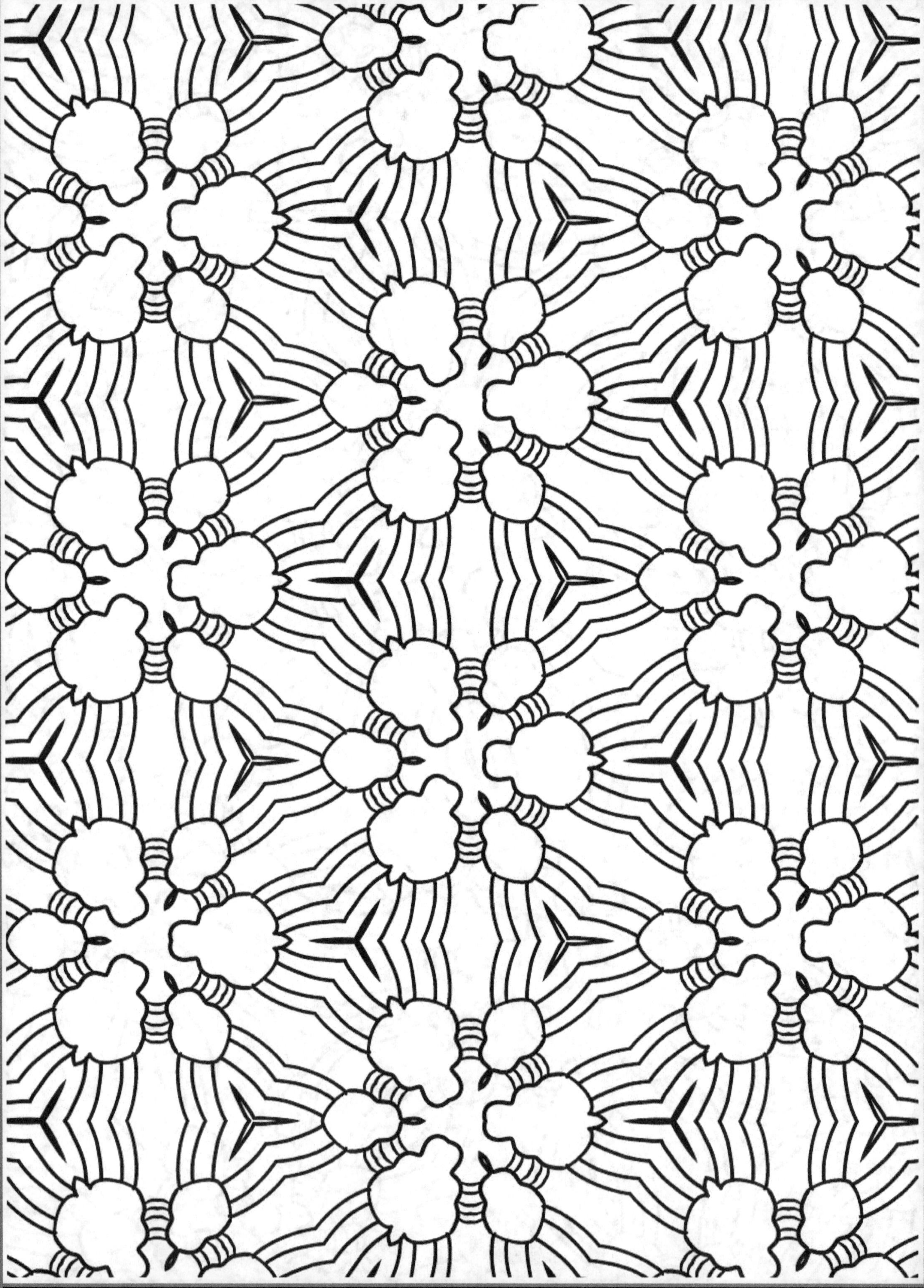

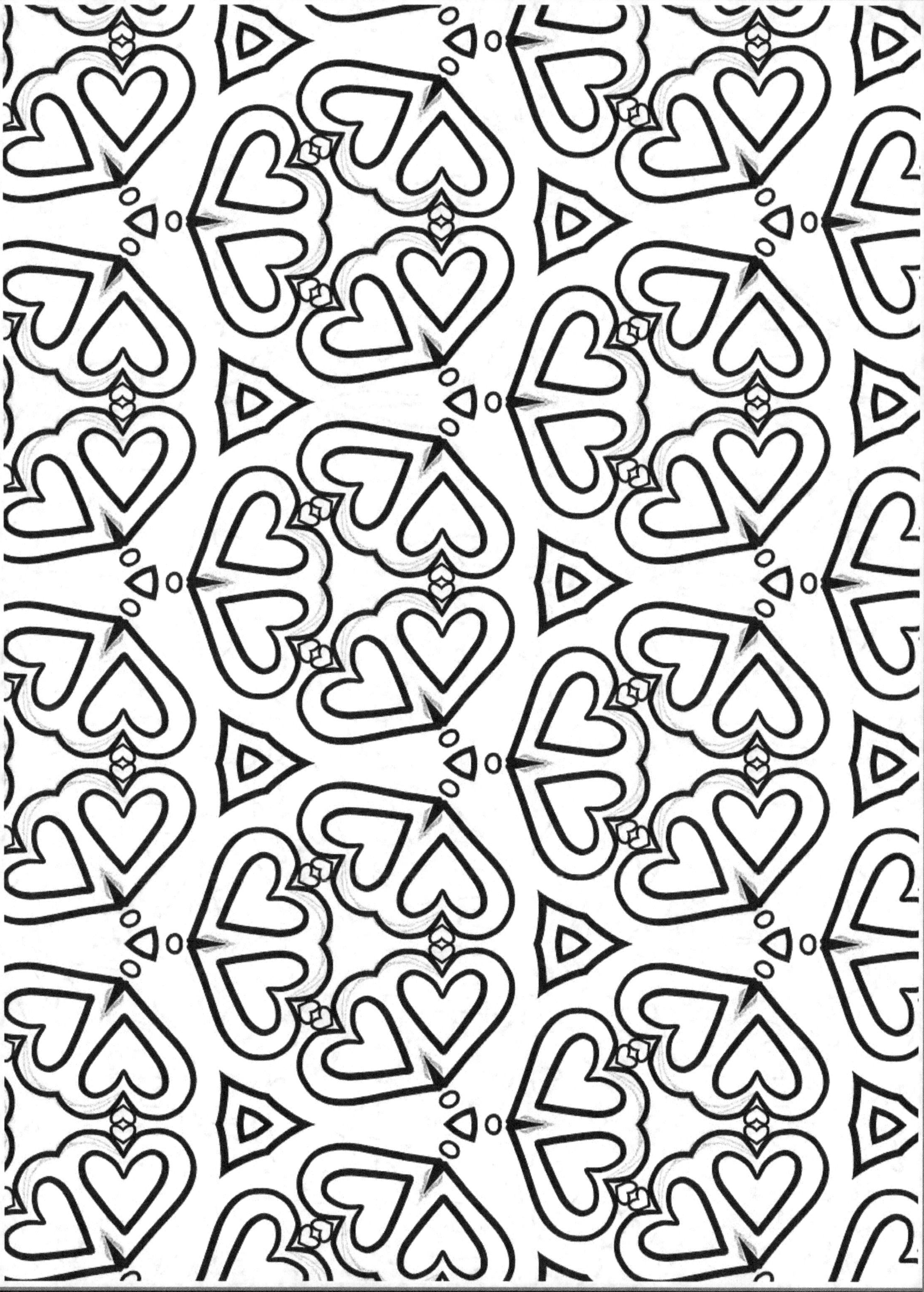

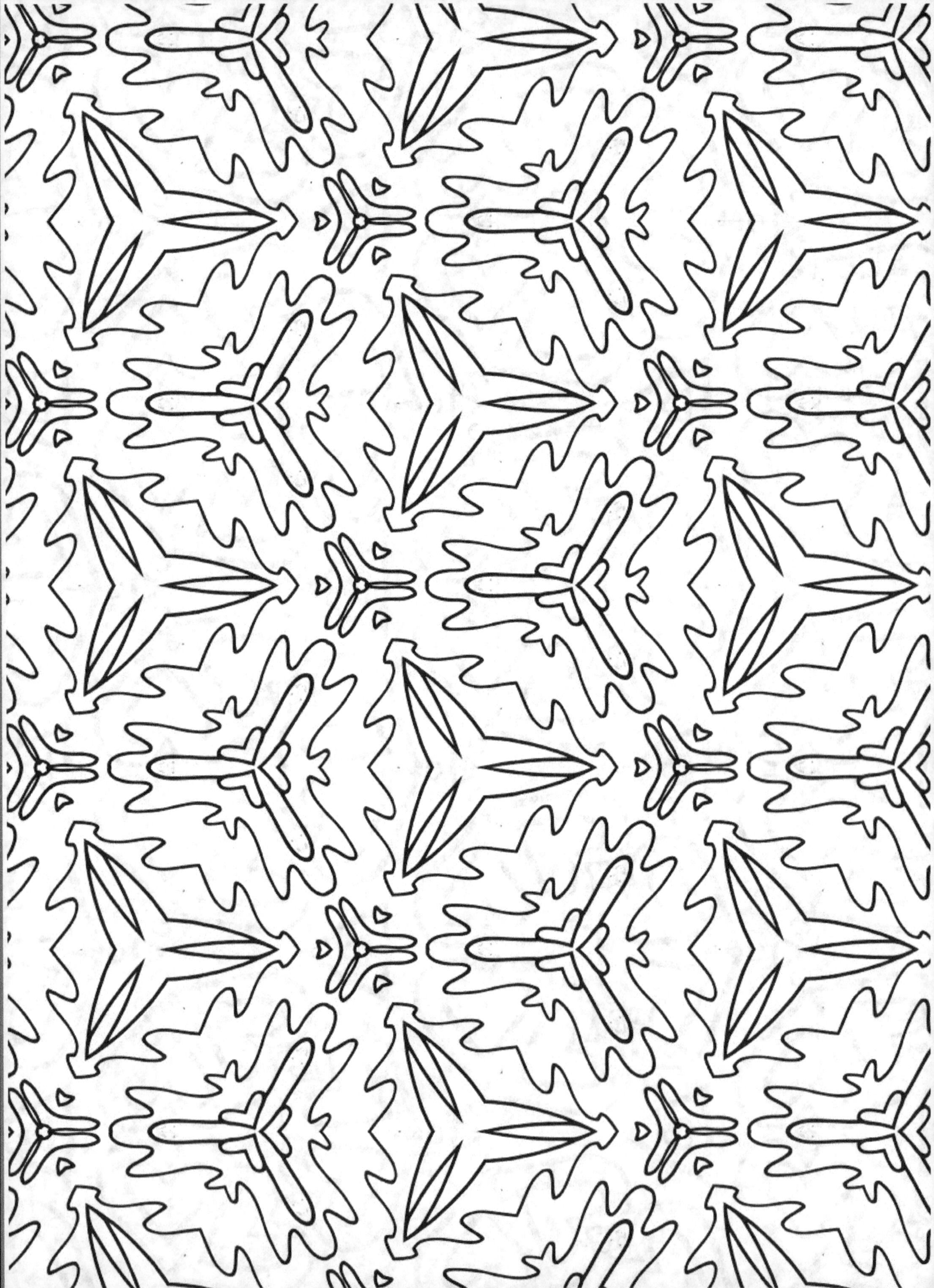

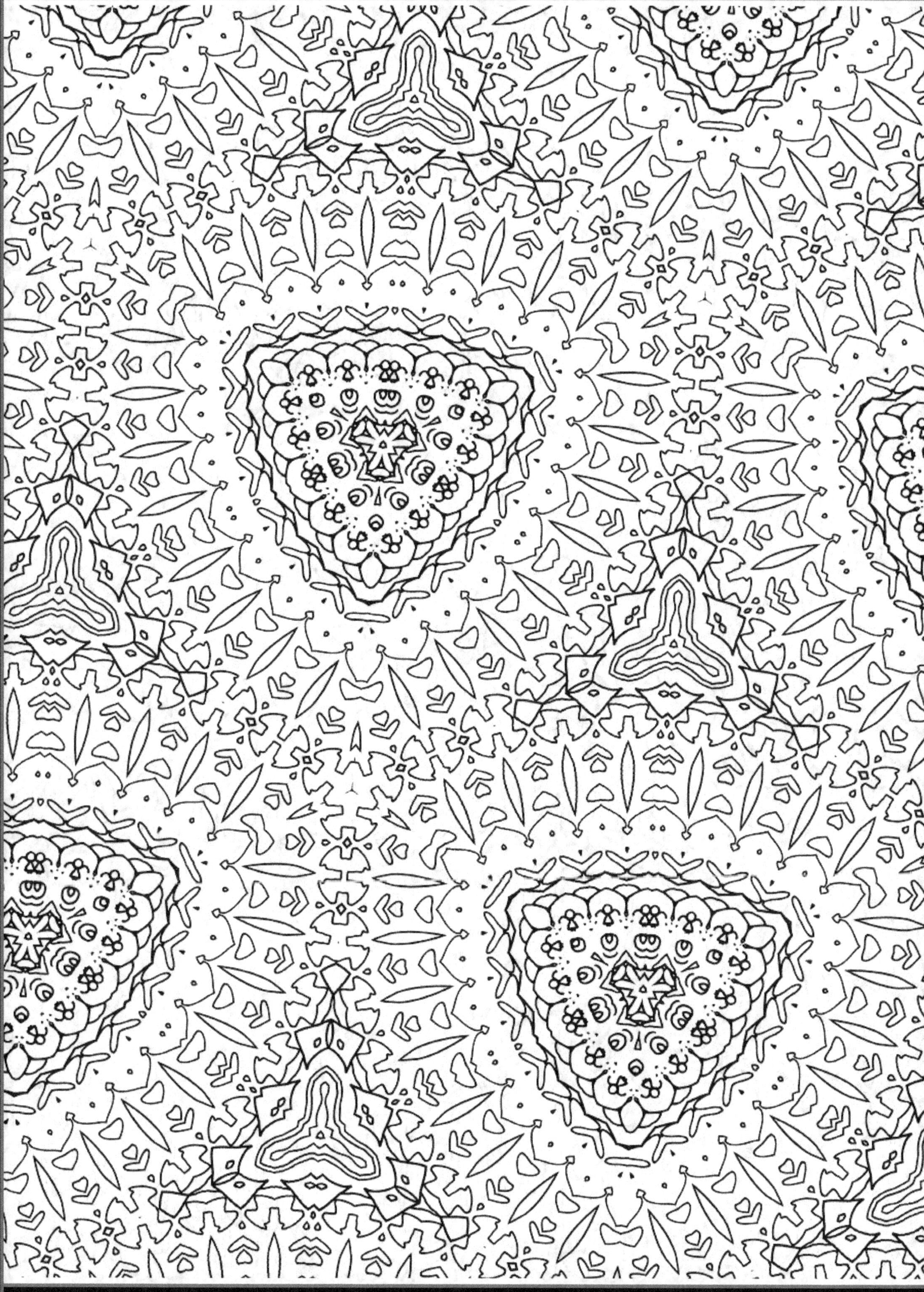

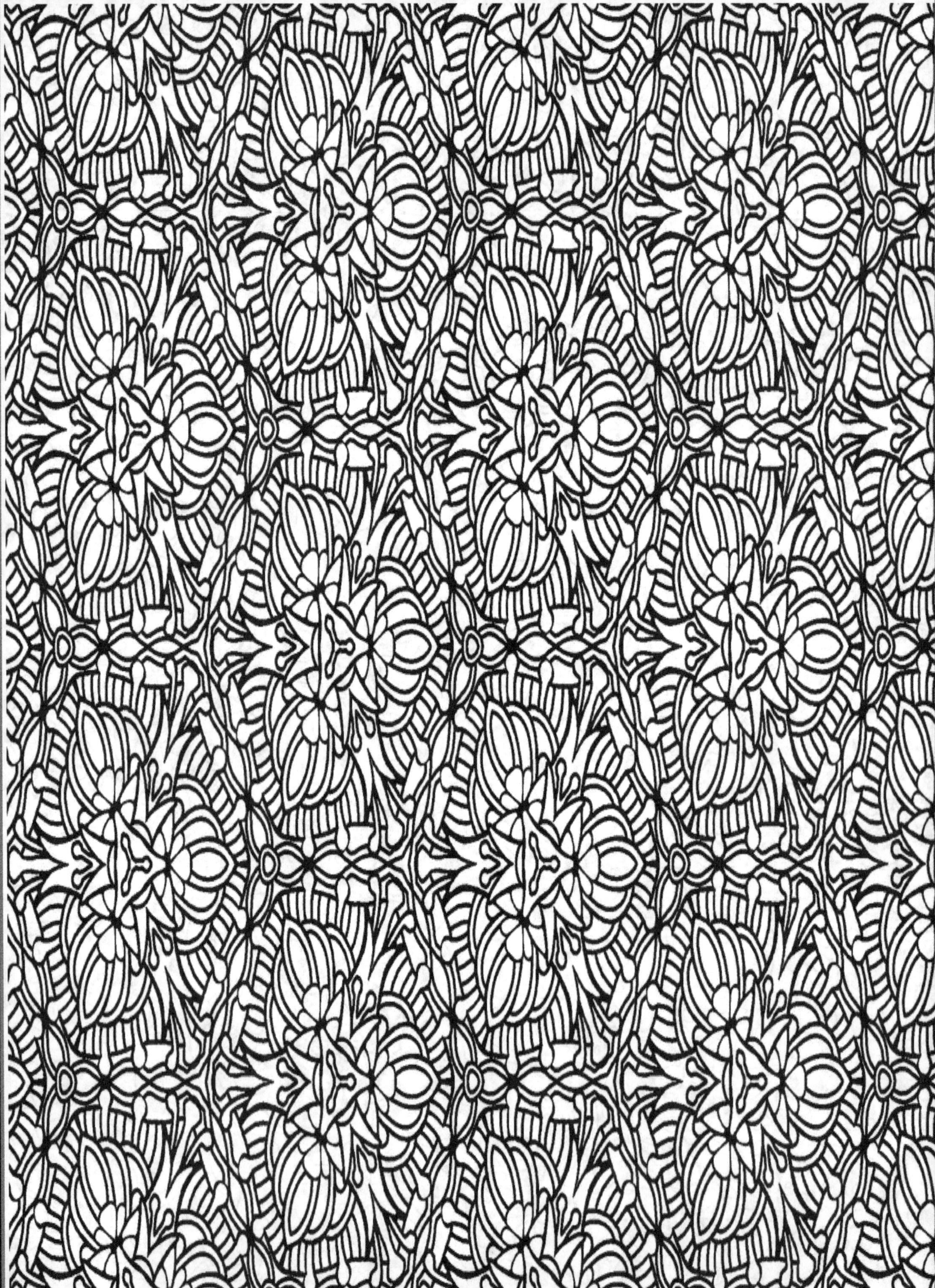

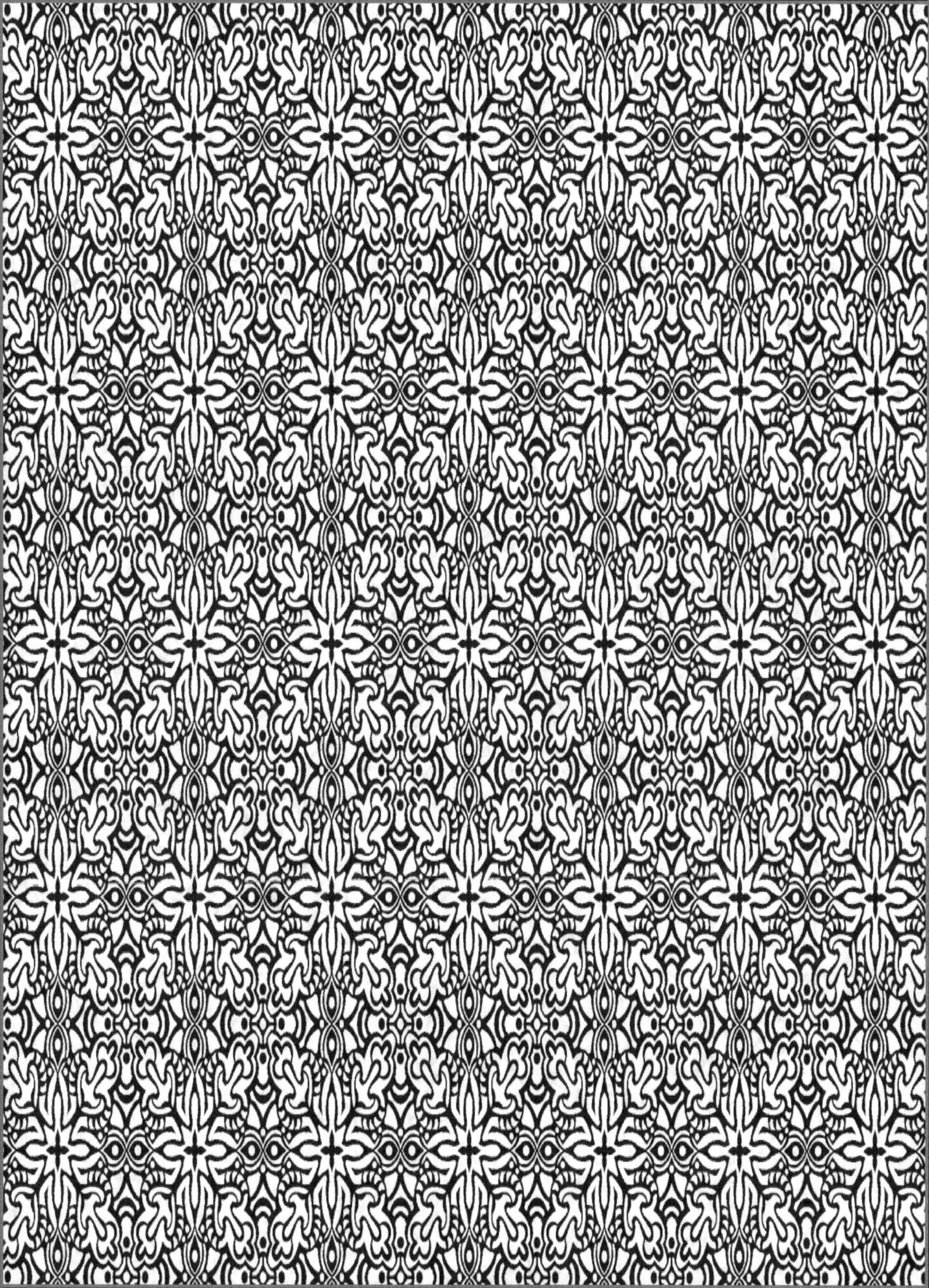

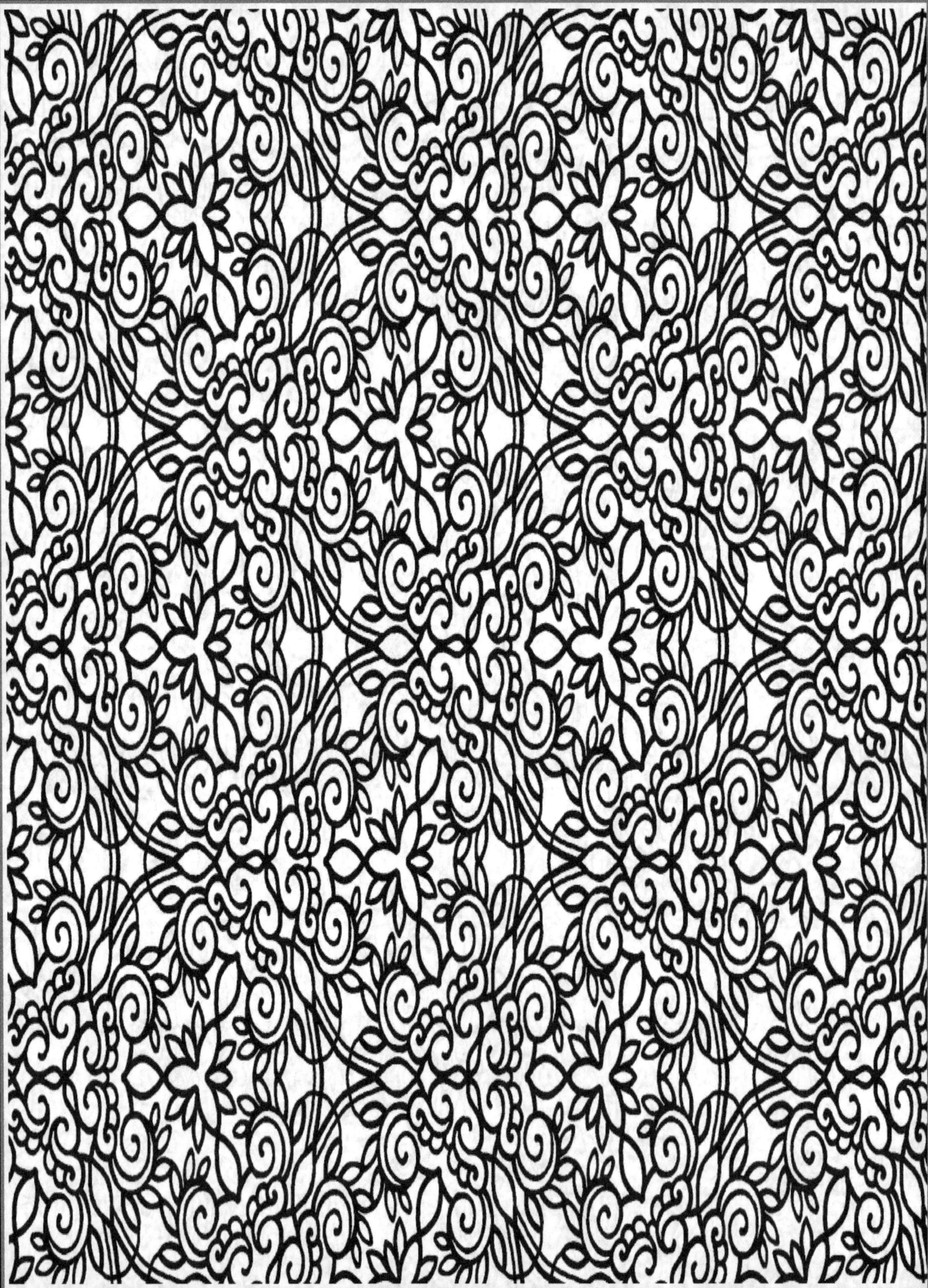

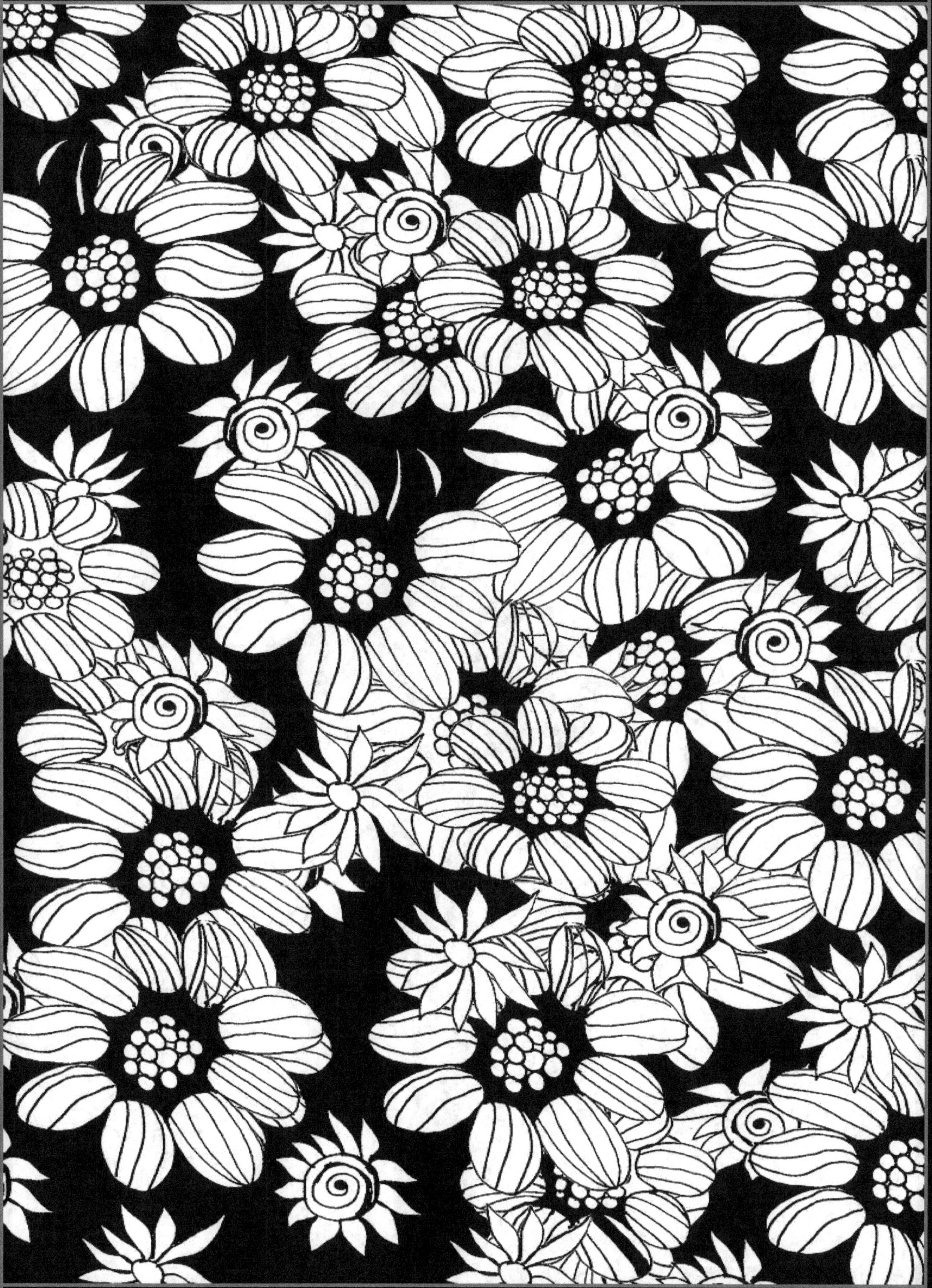

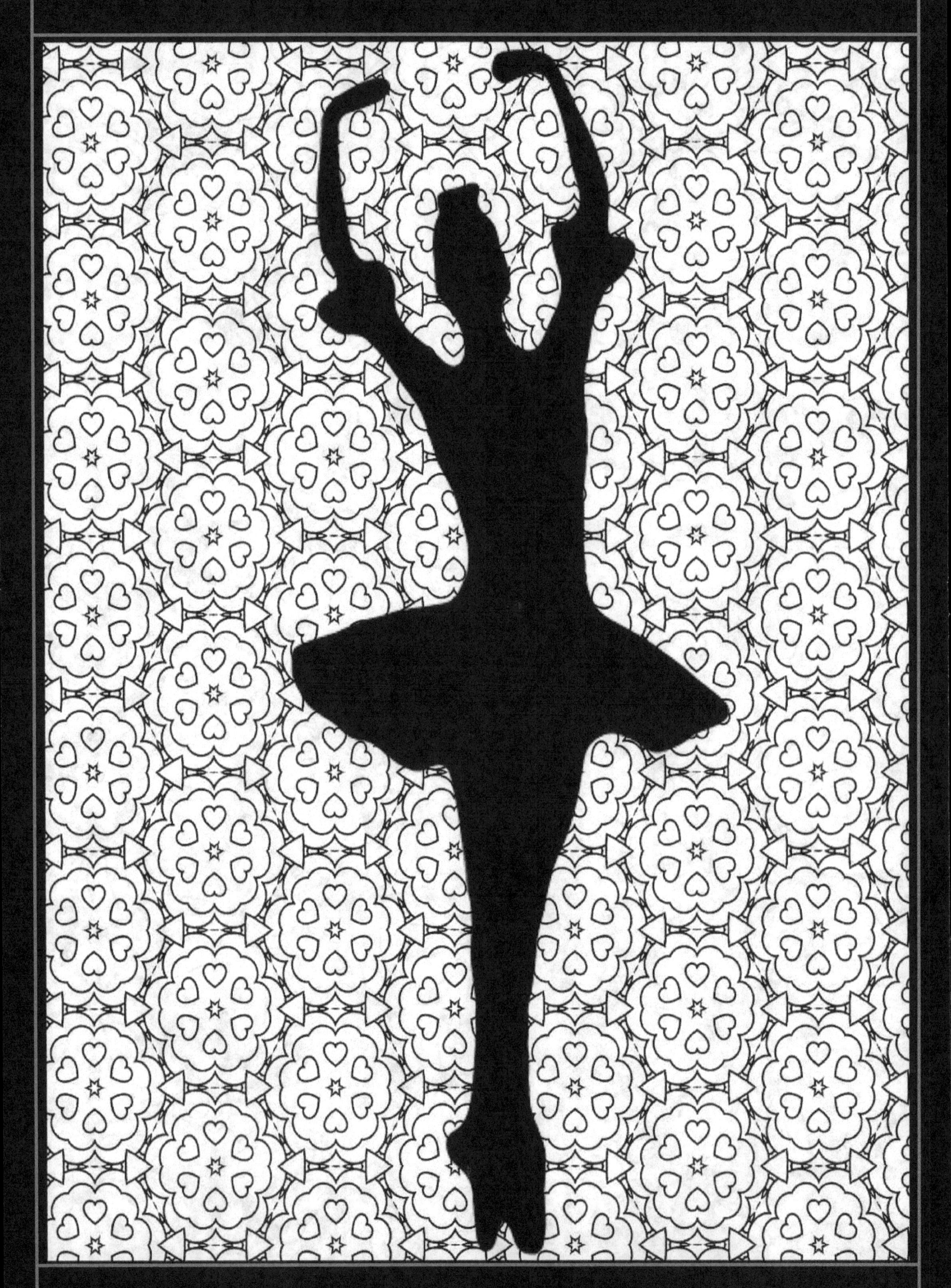

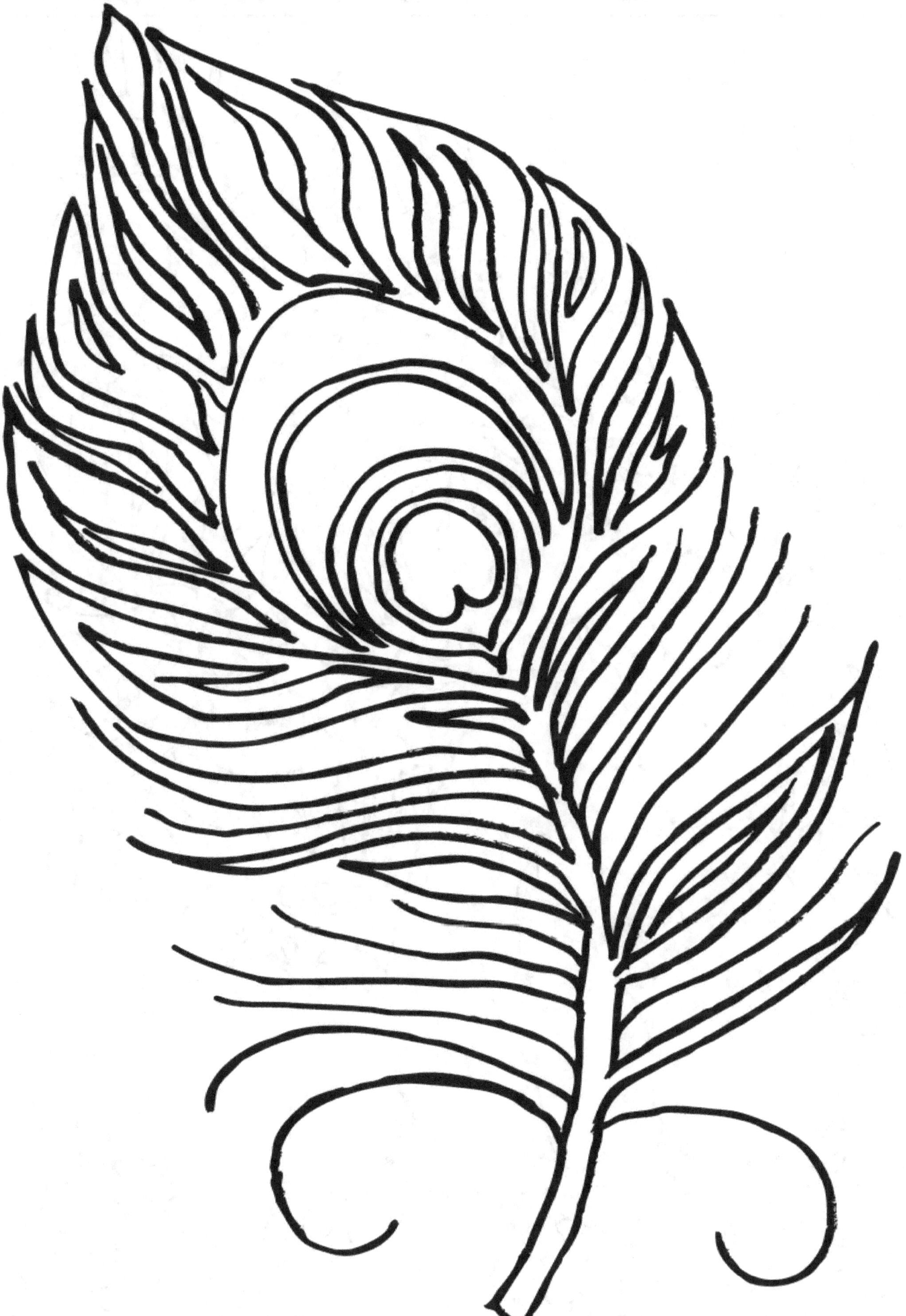

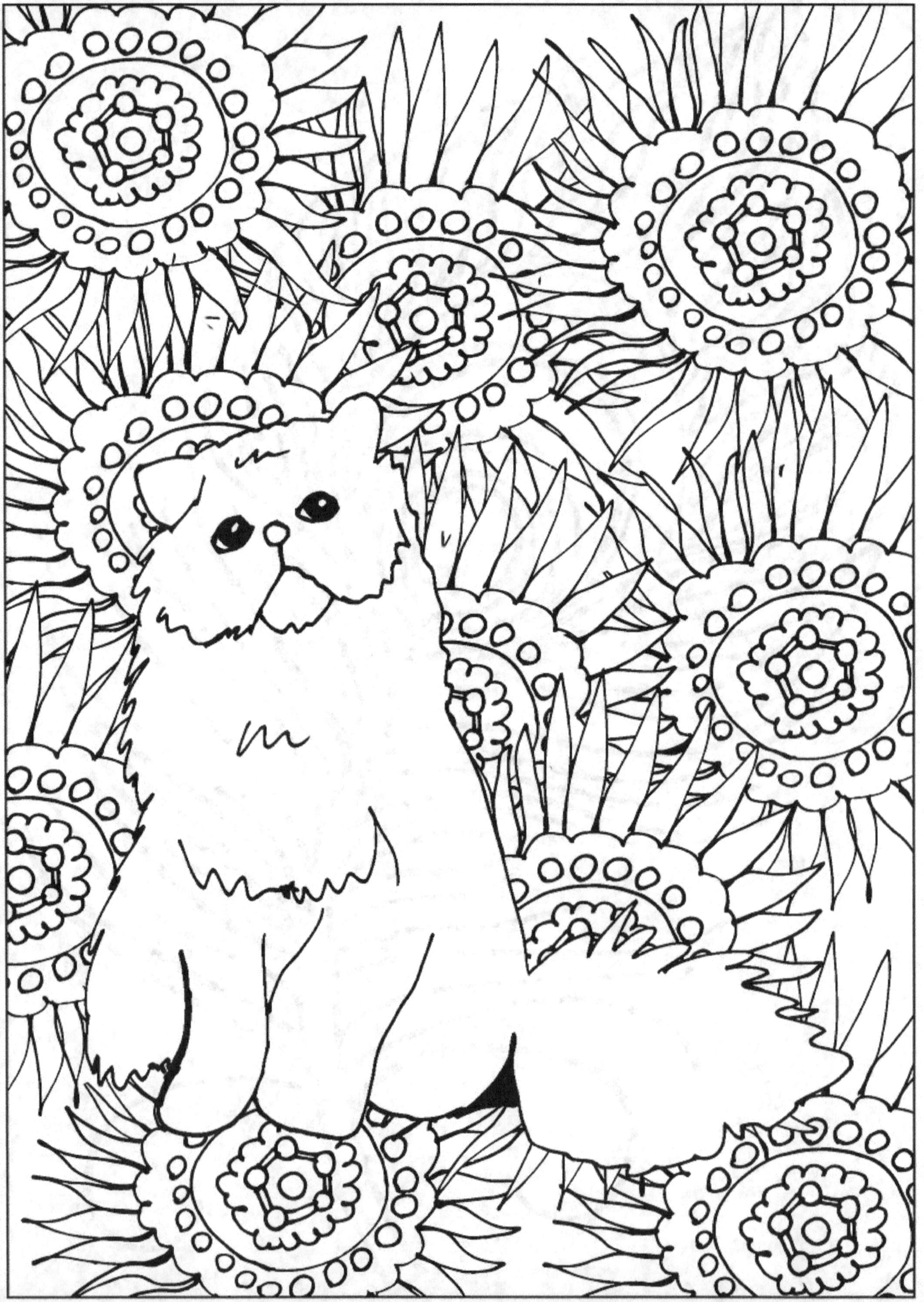

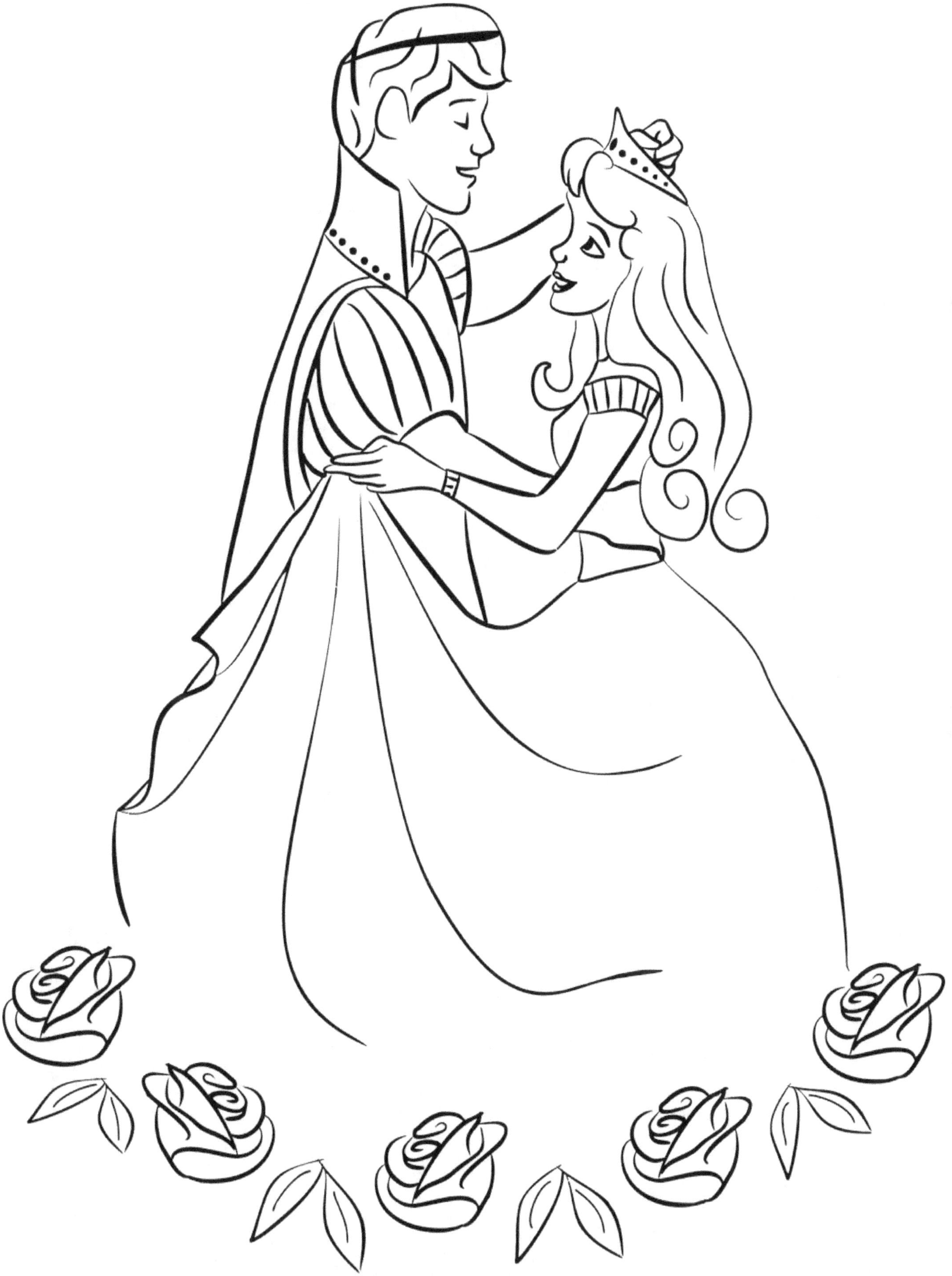

www.ingramcontent.com/pod-product-compliance
Lightning Source LLC
Chambersburg PA
CBHW080854220526
45467CB00008B/2505
* 9 7 8 1 7 1 7 8 6 1 3 6 8 *